Indoctrinating Our Youth

How a U.S. Public School Curriculum Skews the Arab-Israeli Conflict and Islam

Steven Stotsky

CAMERA Monograph Series

A publication of CAMERA,
Committee for Accuracy in Middle East Reporting in America
Boston, Massachusetts

CAMERA, the Committee for Accuracy in Middle East Reporting in America, is a national media-monitoring organization founded in 1982 that works to promote more accurate, balanced and complete coverage of Israel and the Middle East. Aware of the vital role of the mass media in shaping public perception and public policy, CAMERA seeks to educate both journalists and news consumers about the complex issues related to achievement of peace in the Middle East. CAMERA is a non-profit, tax-exempt organization under section 501(c)(3) of the United States Internal Revenue Code.

Published by
The Committee for Accuracy in Middle East Reporting in America
CAMERA
P.O. Box 35040
Boston, MA 02135

Copyright © 2017 by The Committee for Accuracy in Middle East Reporting in America
ISBN 978-0-9661548-9-4

Book design: Emily Regan

Cover Photo: Shutterstock.com

Photos: commons.wikipedia.org with the following exceptions: P. 7 digital artwork by Emily Regan; P. 16, 17 October 24, 2011 Newton school committee meeting screen capture; P. 18 *Indoctrination@Newton* screen capture; P. 25 Palwatch.org; P. 27 *New York Times* video "Challenges in Defining an Israeli-Palestinian Border" screen capture; P. 32 PASSIA class handout; P. 33 scan of class handout; P. 48 scan of *Time Magazine* cover; P. 59 WhiteHouse.gov; P. 61 Brooklyn College Students for Justice in Palestine Facebook page.

Contents

Introduction

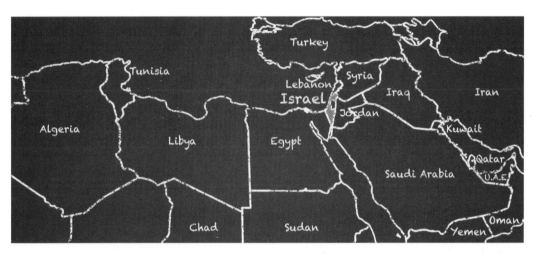

In recent years, the teaching of history in schools has turned toward accounts that give greater recognition to non-Western contributions and beliefs.[1] As part of a decades-long shift away from a study of the past that emphasized the unique contributions of Western culture, educators have endeavored to expand students' knowledge of the Middle East and Islam. The September 11, 2001 attacks on America and growing numbers of Muslim refugees from Middle East conflicts admitted to the U.S. added impetus to this effort.[2]

The shift in emphasis has prompted publishers to substantially revise textbooks and educators to seek new sources of information. The advent of the Internet in the 1990s provided easy access to a wider range of materials, but left individual teachers with the task of critically evaluating them. Not surprisingly, many teachers lacked sufficient background on these complex topics to assess the accuracy of diverse, unvetted sources. The greater latitude in choosing materials has also meant teachers' selections may reflect their own biases. As a result, inaccurate and partisan materials have made their way into some curricula.

Additionally, because history courses in public schools traditionally steered clear of contentious contemporary topics, many school systems have been ill-equipped to address effectively problems that arise from the introduction of biased materials promoting politically-charged agendas.

Reflecting the impact of these broad trends, controversy erupted in 2011 between a group of concerned residents in Newton, Massachusetts and the city's school officials over classroom assignments relating to Islam and the Israeli-Palestinian conflict. In early 2012, the Committee for Accuracy in Middle East Reporting in America (CAMERA) was approached by concerned residents seeking an assessment of a number of school materials. Handouts assigned to 10th graders on the Israeli-Palestinian conflict were among the first items presented and a review showed they contained factual errors and noticeable bias.

For example, a photocopied page from an Internet site called "Flashpoints: Guide to World Conflicts" identified Jerusalem as the capital of Palestine and Tel Aviv as the capital of Israel. These are serious factual errors. Jerusalem is the capital of Israel and there is no state of Palestine. The handout also contained politically-charged statements on "unilateral Israeli policies in the Occupied Territories" and alleged a growing Israeli "influence over American domestic politics and Middle East policy."[3] (See Attachment 1.)

Another handout presented a timeline of the Israeli-Palestinian conflict that omitted any mention of the numerous Arab terrorist attacks inside Israel during the 1970s and 1980s. In fact, the first terrorist attack in Israel or the Palestinian administered territories cited was the first and only mass-fatality attack perpetrated by an Israeli civilian in Israel's history. Given the vastly disproportionate numbers of Palestinian terrorist attacks on Jews, the amplifying of the only such Jewish attack underscores the bias of the handout.

Additionally, a 9th grade history class on Islam had been assigned a chapter from a book titled *A Muslim Primer*,[4] (see Attachment 2) which presented an embellished description of the status of women in Islamic societies without discussion about controversial practices in some Muslim communities.

This first sample of materials being used in Newton classrooms was not, it turned out, an isolated deviation from an otherwise scholarly, sound curriculum. Rather a review of additional items indicated a wider problem in curriculum units devoted to the Israeli-Palestinian conflict and Islam.

This monograph presents a case study of a nationally prominent public school system whose curriculum was compromised by inaccurate accounts of the Israeli-Palestinian conflict and simplistic expositions of Islamic culture. As school systems continue to introduce contemporary, politically contentious topics into their curricula, there are valid concerns that students may be exposed to indoctrination rather than factual, objective accounts.

The purpose here is to provide a careful analysis of what occurred in Newton and to raise awareness of the trends underway. All communities should review the presentation of these subjects in their school systems in order to promote scholarly, accurate materials and to remove factually inaccurate and biased curricula. This monograph focuses only on the units that touch on the Israeli-Palestinian conflict and Islam because these were the objects of concern in the controversy described. The monograph does not examine related topics covered in the world history course like the portrayal of ancient Israel or the history and doctrine of Judaism and Christianity. These could be the subjects of another inquiry. However, no public complaints on curriculum materials have been brought forth to suggest other areas of concern in the Newton High School history curriculum.

1   David Randall, *The Disappearing Continent: A Critique of the Revised Advanced Placement European History Exam,* National Association of Scholars, July 2016. https://www.nas.org/images/documents/NAS_apeh_complete.pdf
Randall writes of changes in the teaching of European History that have meant students no longer learn of "Europe's unique development of the architecture of modern knowledge, which made possible almost every modern form of intellectual inquiry."

2   *International Education and Foreign Languages: Keys to Securing Our Future,* p. 22, The National Academies Press 2016. https://www.nap.edu/read/11841/chapter/4 - 22https://www.nap.edu/read/11841/chapter
The chapter enumerates the increase in funding to Title VI and Fulbright programs directed toward foreign language and area expertise to improve "cultural competencies" in the wake of the 9/11 attacks.

3   Flashpoints: Guide to World Conflicts, was an Internet web site that appears to be no longer active.

4   Ira Zepp, *A Muslim Primer: Beginner's Guide to Islam,* University of Arkansas Press, 2000.

Part 1: An Agenda-Driven History Curriculum

The increased emphasis on contributions of Islamic culture to the modern world is connected to a broader trend that deemphasizes traditional accounts of Western history while increasing students' exposure to non-Western perspectives.[1] Whereas traditional historical accounts teach that Europeans uniquely articulated the ideals of freedom, put them into practice, and created the modern world,[2] contemporary accounts increasingly stress the contributions of other cultures.

The inclusion of other cultural perspectives can provide students with a broader understanding of history. But the enhancement of the stature of other cultures is often accompanied by a critical portrayal of the history and policies of the United States. In the setting of the Middle East, this critical, often negative, scrutiny applies as well to Israel, which is seen as an outpost of Western culture and a continuance of its alleged sins.

Critics of the U.S. and Israel Invited into the Newton Schools

The receptivity to anti-Western perspectives was best dramatized by the visit to Newton South High School in April 2007 of MIT linguistics professor Noam Chomsky, an academic known for his criticism of the United States and antipathy toward the state of Israel. Chomsky was invited by the Social Awareness Club at the school and spoke to an estimated 140 students about the Iraq war.[3]

Local newspapers carried letters and editorials by Newton residents sparring over the appropriateness of the invitation given Chomsky's views, especially those critical of Israel. According to the *Boston Globe*, Student Senate President Dan Groob, who opposed Chomsky's invitation, tried to videotape the event but was ordered outside. Groob called it "horrible and hypocritical" that Chomsky was allowed to speak at the school in a controlled environment, without an opposing viewpoint being offered. Chomsky focused mostly on what he termed the "illegal" American war in Iraq and impressed upon students the notion that a small segment of wealthy elites determines American foreign policy.[4]

Not mentioned during Chomsky's talk was a video[5] of a visit he paid a year earlier in 2006 to Hassan Nasrallah, the leader of Hezbollah, the Iranian-backed Shiite terrorist organization in southern Lebanon.

In that video, Chomsky expressed admiration for the terrorist group and support for its goals. Hezbollah had been responsible for the April 1983 suicide bombing of the U.S. embassy in Lebanon that killed 63 people in the first large-scale Islamist attack on the U.S. It was followed by a suicide truck bombing on October 23, 1983, that killed 241 U.S. Marines serving as peacekeepers in Lebanon. Over the following years, Hezbollah carried out kidnappings, murders and bombings of American, Israeli and Jewish targets, including

Hassan Nasrallah, left, and Noam Chomsky, right

the bombing of a Jewish community center in Argentina that took 85 lives, both Jewish and non-Jewish.[6] In 1997, the U.S. designated Hezbollah a foreign terrorist organization. (Just a month after Chomsky's visit with Hezbollah, the terrorist group launched an unprovoked cross-border attack against Israel, precipitating a five-week war in which over 1000 people, mainly Lebanese, died).

Much of the controversy associated with Chomsky's visit to Newton centered on his denunciations of Israel and his perceived alignment with anti-Semites.[7] Eric Dyer, then a junior at Newton South, recalled encountering extensive anti-Israel sentiment among teachers at the time. In a class discussion in which a teacher condemned Israeli military incursions into Palestinian towns, Dyer objected because there was no mention of Palestinian terrorism. According to Dyer, the teacher censured him for expressing pro-Israel views.[8]

Chomsky was not the first person known for his negative perspective on the U.S. and Israel to be invited to speak to Newton students. In November 2001, two months after the 9/11 attacks, historian Howard Zinn, speaking at Newton North High School, reportedly told students that America's military response in Afghanistan "puts us at the same level as a terrorist."[9]

Some Newton high school students are receptive to this sort of anti-Western and anti-Israel political agenda. A radical political organization called Massachusetts Peace Action has chapters in both Newton high school campuses. This group promotes extreme anti-Israel positions, accusing Israel of scheming to drag the United States into war. The group's website page on the Israeli-Palestinian conflict states,

> "Israel's continued advocacy of a military strike on Iran keeps the region on edge and is the main driver of a threatened U.S.-Iran conflict."[10]

Meanwhile, the group is silent on threats made by the Iranian regime's leaders to erase what it calls the "Zionist entity." The two Newton high schools are the only secondary school chapters featured on the group's web site and the group's board of directors includes a Newton high school student.[11]

Newton Schools and the Harvard Outreach Center

A year after Chomsky's visit to the school, a high school history teacher invited Paul Beran, then director of the Outreach Center at Harvard University's Center for Middle Eastern Studies, to participate in a discussion about the Oslo Peace Process.

Beran was known for promoting the Boycott, Divestment, and Sanctions campaign in the city of Somerville, Massachusetts, and for advocating sanctions against Israel by the Presbyterian Church.[12] He also conducted workshops for teachers where he promoted his political agenda.

The Outreach Center had already received negative publicity for its controversial methods. After the 9/11 attacks, the Massachusetts Board of Education had funded a special seminar for K-12 teachers to learn about Islamic history and the Middle East. The outreach coordinator at the Outreach Center had been selected to organize the seminar. In their review of the seminar, officials from the Massachusetts Department of Education were shocked at what they found. They criticized the program for "ethical violations" that included "unacceptable practices" of inculcating religious practice in a public school classroom.[13]

A slide presentation available in 2011-2012 on the Outreach Center's website revealed the political advocacy woven into educational materials in workshops for teachers. The presentation laid out a number of key points to teach about the conflict.

1. It emphasized treating the Israeli-Palestinian conflict as simply a land or border dispute, while dismissing the possibility of any other cause – for example, a religious one – as an "unsophisticated" viewpoint. [14]

2. It portrayed the Palestinians as the indigenous people of the land, while obscuring the Jewish historical connection. One slide featured four chronological maps alleging to document the expansion of Jewish-controlled territory and the corresponding elimination of Palestinian territory. In fact, all the land shown in the maps had been part of the Turkish Ottoman Empire for 400 years until 1917. After World War I, the territory was part of a British administered League of Nations mandate for the

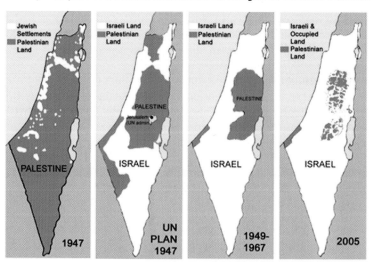

creation of a Jewish national home. However, the maps convey the impression of a once existing Palestinian Arab state. There has never been any such state.[15]

3. It depicted Palestinians as victims, unaccountable for their own decisions that might have led to their current predicament. This too was presented as a "sophisticated" viewpoint. One slide purporting to be "sophisticating" (sophisticated) alleged that "Israel is hegemon." It discredited as "unsophisticated" notions like "Palestinians as terrorists."[16]

The Harvard Outreach Center presentation steered participants toward numerous anti-Zionist films and books, especially works by Jewish anti-Zionists.[17]

Among the films promoted on the website was *Occupation 101*,[18] a film featuring such well-known anti-Zionists as Noam Chomsky, Alison Weir, and Richard Falk. The themes expressed in the film echoed the Center's advocacy. The film analogizes Israel's policies to apartheid in South Africa. It denies the Jewish people's connection to their historic home, and incorporates classical anti-Jewish religious imagery and the anti-historical notion of a "Palestinian" Christ. The Palestinians are viewed only as victims. Palestinian violence is justified as a natural response to injustice.[19]

The Outreach Center also recommended to teachers a controversial textbook titled the *Arab World Studies Notebook* (AWSN). A review of the AWSN by the American Jewish Committee (AJC) found that the textbook "appears largely designed to advance the anti-Israel and propagandistic views of the Notebook's two sponsors, the Middle East Policy Council (MEPC) and Arab World and Islamic Resources (AWAIR), to an audience of teachers who may not have the resources and knowledge to assess this text critically."[20] The AJC report noted the irony that "the *Notebook* critiques other educational materials for being Eurocentric, yet it provides students with a completely Muslim-centered perspective."[21]

The AJC report concluded, "The Notebook is replete with factual errors, inaccuracies, and misrepresentations.[22] In addition to pervasive typographical errors, there is an almost total lack of citation,[23] making reference-checking exceptionally difficult, if not impossible."[24]

An example of the *Notebook*'s bias is evident in a chapter on "An Arab City," which presents Jerusalem as the "ancestral home" of the Palestinians that was usurped by Israel. It states that "Westerners know Jerusalem's deep associations with Judaism and Christianity... However, Islam's religious ties with the Holy city are equally long and much deeper."[25]

In fact, Islam emerged in the 7th century C.E., over 16 centuries after Jerusalem became the religious and political center for the Jewish nation, and six centuries after Jerusalem's religious importance was established for Christians.

The book's section on the Palestinians begins with the assertion, for which there is no historical basis, that, "Some Palestinians can trace their ancestry directly to the Canaanites who lived in Palestine centuries before the Hebrews claimed part of it."[26]

Another example of the Notebook's extreme bias is its contention that a Jewish conspiracy is behind the allegedly poor image of Arabs and Islam in America: "Why is it Hollywood has been able to malign Arabs with almost complete impunity? Is there a Jewish conspiracy to promote a negative image of Arabs in cinema? Indeed Jews have been prominent in the American film industry and American Jews tend to be supportive of Israel. Meanwhile the emergence of the Israeli film industry with ties to America...has clearly contributed to the increase in racist portrayals of Arabs in cinema."[27]

In fact, the Israeli film industry has a notable repertoire containing numerous works that critically scrutinize Israeli policy and are sympathetic to the Palestinians.[28] Reviews of these films reveal that many are biased in favor of the Palestinians to such a degree that they promote unsubstantiated accusations and include false claims reflecting negatively on Israel.[29]

After being alerted to the Outreach Center's workshops in late 2012, CAMERA exposed the biased and inaccurate information disseminated in the workshops.[30] (See Attachment 3.) Shortly thereafter, Beran left and eventually took another position at Harvard,[31] and the Outreach Center shifted its emphasis away from the Israeli-Palestinian conflict to other cultural and political issues in the Middle East. A spokesperson for Harvard's Center for Middle Eastern Studies later told a researcher from a group evaluating Newton school curriculum materials that the Center "disavowed any connection to any such materials that may have been distributed to teachers."[32]

When questioned in 2013 about Beran's influence over the teaching of Islam and the Israeli-Palestinian conflict, Newton's School Superintendent David Fleishman stated that the Oslo discussion was the only interaction that had occurred between Newton teachers and the Harvard Outreach Center.[33] And a 10th grade World History teacher at Newton South High School corroborated the statement, saying that Beran played no role in his selection of curriculum materials.[34]

However, these statements were contradicted by the Outreach Center's own website, which proclaimed that Beran conducted a follow-up session with 80 Newton teachers on April 30, 2010, during which he instructed them on how to teach about the Israeli-Palestinian conflict.[35] And a local community newspaper, *The Jewish Advocate*, reported in 2012 that Newton South High School World History teacher Sean Turley had "sought help from the Center when he designed a 10th grade lesson plan about the Israeli/Palestinian conflict." Turley acknowledged that he had used the plan for three years.[36]

1   David Randall, *The Disappearing Continent*, National Association of Scholars, June 2016. https://www.nas.org/images/documents/NAS_apeh_complete.pdf.

2   Ibid, p. 2.

3   *Boston Globe*, April 11, 2007. http://archive.boston.com/bostonglobe/regional_editions/globe_west/west/2007/04/protesters_decr.html

4   Ibid.

5   https://www.youtube.com/watch?v=-WAP2S6rSoY

6   *Jerusalem Post*, July 18, 2016. http://www.jpost.com/Diaspora/Today-in-history-Argentina-looks-for-justice-460711

7   Chomsky penned an essay "Some Elementary Comments on the Rights of Freedom of Expression" in 1980. This included a defense of Holocaust denier Robert Faurisson. The essay was included as a forward to Faurisson's book. https://chomsky.info/19801011

8   Interview conducted by Steven Stotsky of former Newton South student Eric Dyer, August 2016.

9   *Boston Herald*, Nov. 21, 2011.

10   Massachusetts Peace Action. http://masspeaceaction.org/learn/palestine-israel

11   Ibid, http://masspeaceaction.org/campus-student/

12   Reported in *Harvard's Middle East Outreach Center Headed by BDS Activist,* CAMERA, Dec. 13, 2011. Beran boasted of forming a coalition with an anti-Israel group, Jewish Voice for Peace, claiming "it helped the PC (USA) to deal more forcefully with the criticism it has and continues to receive from Zionist groups and their ilk."

13   CBN news, Public Schools Teach the ABCs about Islam, Oct. 9. 2008.

14   Mitchell Bard for example offers a sharply different viewpoint in his book, "Death to the Infidels: Radical Islam's War Against the Jews" St. Martin's Press, 2007.

15   The original source of these maps is the PLO Information Office. Many versions of these maps circulate widely.

16   Slide from 2011 Harvard University Center for Middle Eastern Studies website, titled, "Sophisticating."

17   PowerPoint slides for the workshop were originally available on the Outreach Center's website. They have since been removed.

18   Steven Stotsky, *Film Review: Occupation 101,* CAMERA, Jan. 5, 2008.

19   The film opens with the lines: "Any violence by a large population is not because the people is more violent than any other. It's an alarm, it's a sign, it's a signal that something is wrong in the treatment of this population."

20   *Propaganda, Proselytizing and Public Education: A Critique of the Arab World Studies Notebook,* prepared by Doran Arik, published by the American Jewish Committee, 2005.

21   Ibid, p.3.

22   Stanley Kurtz, "Saudi in the Classroom," *National Review,* July 25, 2007.

23   An example of the lack of scholarly citation is the inflated American Muslim population figure provided by the book (6 million in 1998 and noting it was larger than the Jewish population). In an exchange with William Bennetta, editor of *The Textbook League,* AWSN editor Audrey Shabbas cited unsubstantiated figures from television programs as her source of the population figure. In contrast, population surveys by reputable organizations (for example, Pew) estimated the American Muslim population at 1.8-4 million in 2010. http://www.freerepublic.com/focus/news/1018887/posts

24   Ibid, p.8.

25   *Arab World Studies Notebook,* 1989 edition. p. 61.

26   Ibid, p. 247.

27   Ibid, p. 285.

28   In 2005, the Sundance Film Festival in Colorado, a major venue for independent films, featured nine Israeli films, all of which were sympathetic to the Palestinians and none of which could be characterized as denigrating Arabs.

29   CAMERA's website www.camera.org contains over a dozen film reviews that support this finding.

30   CAMERA, "Harvard's Middle East Center Headed by BDS Supporter," Dec. 13 2011. http://www.camera.org/index.asp?x_context=2&x_outlet=118&x_article=

31   Beran recently was appointed as executive director of SHARIAsource, a newly created online platform designed to provide content and context on Islamic law. It is part of Harvard Law School's Islamic Legal Studies Program.

32   Verity Educate, *Middle East Curricula in Newton Public Schools,* p. 4.

33   *Boston Globe,* State Affirms School Curriculum After Protests," Nov. 7, 2013.

34   Interview with Hillel Stavis Aug. 9, 2016, in which Stavis, a former school principal and bookstore owner in Cambridge, MA, recounted his conversation with Newton South High School history teacher James Rinaldi.

35   The full statement reads as follows: "The Outreach Center is working with the Newton city high schools to develop new resources to use in the classroom to teach the Palestinian/Israeli conflict. Paul Beran CMESOC Director presented to 80 history teachers from Newton Public Schools on approaches and resources for teaching about the Palestinian/Israeli conflict. The approach offered provides an inclusive way to allow a wide variety of historical voices to be learned from in the conflict. It then, approaches the gathering of information for presentation in the classroom around resources that focus on the five Oslo Peace Process problem areas of refugees, resources, borders, Jerusalem and settlements..." https://web.archive.org/web/20100708082509/http:/cmes.hmdc.harvard.edu/outreach/news/newtonschools

36   *Jewish Advocate,* Feb. 17, 2012.

Part 2: Curriculum Controversy in Newton, Massachusetts

Reading Assignment from a Controversial Textbook

The controversy over the teaching of the Israeli-Palestinian conflict and Islam in Newton erupted in the fall of 2011 when Tony Pagliuso, a Newton school parent, discovered his daughter had been assigned to read an inflammatory article for a unit covering the Israeli-Palestinian conflict. The article stated:

> "Over the past four decades, women have been active in the Palestinian resistance movement. Several hundred have been imprisoned, tortured, and killed by Israeli occupation forces."[1]

The offending passage was from the *Arab World Studies Notebook,* which had been recommended by the Harvard Outreach Center.[2] There is no factual merit to the outrageous assertion made in the article, nor does the *Notebook* provide any backup for its false claims.

According to Pagliuso, when he brought the issue up with his daughter's teacher, his concerns were rejected and he was told that the material was appropriate for the class.[3] He received a similar response from the head of Newton South's Social Studies Department. In a meeting with the school principal, Pagliuso recalled that he felt patronized. According to Pagliuso, the principal taunted him, stating that "next year we're going to be studying some things that are going to be even more upsetting to you about the Israeli-Palestinian conflict."[4]

After a local newspaper reported on the incident,[5] an ad-hoc group formed in Newton to examine the materials that were used to teach about Islam and the Israeli-Palestinian conflict. The group set up meetings with school officials and began regularly to attend school committee meetings to voice their concerns about problematic curriculum materials.[6]

In June 2012, the superintendent and the Newton School Committee asserted that articles[7] copied from the Arab World Studies Notebook had been removed from the curriculum.[8] The Newton Public Schools published an official statement about the Arab World Studies Notebook controversy. It claimed that "The teacher highlighted a controversial statement in the reading and noted that it was a biased perspective..." The official statement reaffirmed that the book was no longer used at Newton South High School after a review during the winter of 2011-

2012, and that Newton North High School followed suit in the spring of 2012.[9] (See Attachment 4.) However, the Jewish News Service reported that downloadable lesson plans for a Newton South 9th grade class still included passages from the problematic textbook in October 2012.[10]

Notably, the Newton Public Schools statement did not take issue with the factual errors in the textbook, instead finding that "while it included primary sources that were of value to some faculty, there was a general sense that the materials were outdated."[11]

The Battle Between the School Committee and the Ad-Hoc Group of Concerned Citizens

The ad-hoc group that formed after the exposure of the error-ridden reading assignment began its activities in earnest at a school committee meeting on October 24, 2011. Thirteen members of the ad-hoc group expressed their concerns with the curriculum. The superintendent acknowledged that some materials were factually flawed, but defended their use by claiming that it was important to provide students with a "balanced perspective," a phrase he repeated four times.[12] He added that he was familiar with an American Jewish Committee study that severely criticized the *Arab World Studies Notebook*.[13]

Subsequently, other school officials endorsed the superintendent's view, contending that inaccurate materials helped to "sharpen students' critical thinking skills."[14] Members of the ad-hoc group disagreed, countering that students lacking sufficient knowledge in the subject would not be able to distinguish facts from falsehoods.

Hillel Stavis speaking at school committee meeting

One member of the group who spoke at the meeting, Hillel Stavis, a former school principal, criticized the poor scholarly content of the material and questioned the value of assigning counterfactual readings to young, impressionable students.[15]

Superintendent Fleishman speaking at school committee meeting

School committee members reacted negatively to the ad-hoc group's comments. Expressing his concern with parental involvement in school curricula, Newton School Committee Vice-Chair Matt Hills told a local newspaper reporter that he knew of only a "handful" of residents, "a tiny, tiny number of people" voicing concern over "some unidentified bias." According to Hills, "academic freedom is at stake." He added, "and by the way there's not the slightest notion that there's a problem with the curriculum."[16]

Subsequently, members of the ad-hoc group managed to gain access to additional curriculum materials through private contacts with parents and students. They were troubled to find additional information that seemed unscholarly and biased.[17]

At school committee meetings during the Fall of 2012, members of the ad-hoc group continued to demand redress of their grievances concerning the curriculum. They urged, for example, that an objectionable book (*A Muslim Primer*) be removed due to its scholarly deficiencies in portraying the status of women in Islamic societies.[18] While allowed to speak at the meetings, the group complained that their concerns fell on deaf ears.

Meetings became increasingly contentious. In a letter published in local newspapers, Hills accused members of the ad-hoc group of "McCarthyesque" behavior at school committee meetings.[19]

Members of the ad-hoc group repeatedly urged they be given full access to curricular materials related to the Middle East. However, school officials[20] and the school committee[21] effectively barred access to curriculum materials by ignoring requests from the ad-hoc group. A school official sent one member of the ad-hoc group a letter requesting a payment of $3643, stating that it would be needed to cover the cost of collecting the requested materials.[22] (See Attachment 5.) Additionally, an email sent by Hills to another school committee member stated that the school committee had instructed the superintendent and his curriculum team not to comply with requests to collect and provide curricular materials, even in the case of a Freedom of Information Act request.[23]

```
From:           "Matt Hills ◁▬▬▬▬▬▷
To:             "Brian Yates'" ◁▬▬▬▬▷,
                ◁▬▬▬▬▷
Copies to:      ◁▬▬▬▷
Subject:        Curriculum
Date sent:      Sun, 8 Jul 2012 22:27:12 -0400


Brian (copy to Claire),
I want to quickly follow-up on the voicemail and email that I left for you Thursday. Feel free to call me if you'd
like to talk about this more (my home is▬▬▬▬ and my office is▬▬▬▬).
We have spoken to David about questions regarding the "controversy" surrounding the history class in the high
schools. This was an issue dealt with early last fall and has long since ceased to be a concern for almost every
person who has weighed in on the issue.
As a matter of policy (which is why Claire and I spoke to David about curriculum requests), we have asked
David and the NPS team not to collect and disseminate curriculum information for this or any other course
other than to the extent it is normally distributed to students. We do not feel there is any policy issue involved
(ie a systematically biased curriculum) and will not start down a path that could politicize curriculum decisions.
In any event, there is a FOIA request outstanding that, if pursued, will lead to the NPS compiling certain
curriculum information. Given the policy issue and given the FOIA request, we have asked David to avoid
compiling and distributing curriculum for this or any course, including the request that you sent to him.
```

Email shown in the film *Indoctrination@Newton*

The unresponsiveness to requests for access to curriculum materials exacerbated an already adversarial atmosphere, turning the issue of access to school materials into a focal point of the ad-hoc group's grievances.

Parents for Excellence in Newton Schools (PENS),[24] an organization formed by a parent who had separated from the ad-hoc group, created a website in 2012 to document the meetings with school officials as well as discussions and analyses of the classroom materials.

In July 2012, a contentious meeting took place between PENS and a deputy superintendent.[25] In a letter sent to the Newton School Department and the Mayor's Office recapping the meeting, PENS claimed that the deputy superintendent "indicated that it is acceptable for students to use material with factual inaccuracies" in order to "sharpen student's critical thinking skills" and that "there is no need to review materials used in controversial or sensitive subjects because 'we trust our teachers.'" The letter also cited the deputy superintendent stating that, "neither parents nor anyone else was permitted to view any material used by students."[26]

Other Groups Enter the Fray

As the battle intensified between the sides, local activist groups entered the fray. Americans for Peace and Tolerance (APT), a Boston-area organization that exposes bias in school systems,[27] rallied concerned Newton residents to attend school committee meetings.

APT placed provocative advertisements in local newspapers publicizing examples of the distorted materials used in Newton schools. One ad published in October 2013 asked "What are Newton Students Really Learning?" It listed materials that "demonize Israel and America while glorifying Islam." The ad stirred up controversy because it called on outraged citizens to call the mayor's office and vice-chair of the school, and provided the vice-chair's personal phone number.[28] (See Attachment 6.) While his phone number was listed publicly on the City of Newton's website, its inclusion in the ad further intensified the controversy.

19

APT's activities generated friction with several well-established Jewish organizations in the Boston area. The Boston chapters of the Anti-Defamation League (ADL), the Jewish Community Relations Council (JCRC), and the Combined Jewish Philanthropies (CJP) initially sided with the school committee and officials.[29] In a joint statement issued on November 6, 2013, they publicly rebuked APT, declaring that after a careful review of the materials they had determined that APT's allegations lacked merit.[30] However, they did not publicize their own review of all the controversial materials. It is also not clear how they got the materials to review.[31]

On November 7, 2013, the *Boston Globe* reported that a Newton parent had submitted a 174-page complaint to the State Board of Education alleging that the curriculum

> violated the separation of church and state by spending an "inordinate" amount of time on Islam, and at too high a level of detail. It also alleged that class materials contained anti-Israel, anti-Semitic, racist, and false information, and pointed specifically to passages from *A Muslim Primer, Arab World Studies Notebook,* and a website called "Flashpoints."[32]

According to *The Globe,* state education officials investigated the issue and found "no violation of education law, regulation or policy has occurred with regard to the specific concern(s)" that were raised.[33] (See Attachment 7.)

On December 30, 2013, the ADL followed up its earlier joint statement with a response to APT's allegations that provided more specifics.[34] The ADL position seemed to shift somewhat, concurring with APT that some of the materials were problematic and should not be used.[35] The ADL noted that *Arab World Studies Notebook* had been removed from the school and while agreeing that "Flashpoints: Guide to World Conflicts"[36] was not a credible source, the ADL asserted it too was no longer in use. The ADL also addressed the question of the school's use of *A Muslim Primer: Beginner's Guide to Islam* and advised against further use of the book, but stopped short of demanding its removal. While the ADL's report summarized its findings on the items publicized by APT, there is no indication that the ADL conducted a comprehensive review of all Newton materials used to teach about Islam and the Israeli-Palestinian conflict.

The major Jewish organizations' position continued to shift in 2013 and 2014. In a February 2014 letter to the local Jewish newspaper, the leadership of the Jewish Community Relations Council (JCRC) demonstrated a more nuanced position than its initial one. While it continued to criticize APT for its advertisements and for "attacking the ADL for its leadership on behalf of our community,"[37] the JCRC acknowledged there might be problems with the school materials and offered to meet with parents whose children brought home objectionable materials from school. (See Attachment 8.)

The JCRC suggested that the school committee –"as an elected body representing the voters of Newton – could put this entire chapter to rest by publicly addressing the ongoing allegations once and for all" and further added, "it would benefit the entire community if they would provide a public accounting about how curriculum is developed and how and where materials are approved for classroom distribution."[38]

Review of Newton Curriculum Commissioned

Recognizing the importance of a scholarly assessment of the curriculum materials, some members of the ad-hoc group asked a Florida-based academic service called Verity Educate to evaluate the content of the materials they had been able to obtain from students up to that point, a total of 26 items.

In September 2014, Verity Educate produced a comprehensive report[39] that was highly critical of the materials. The 153-page report identified numerous examples of shoddy scholarship, plagiarism, and information copied from anti-Semitic websites. An executive summary of the report states that, "There has been a demonstrated lack of subject matter expertise in the creation and oversight of these materials and the vast majority of materials used do not originate from authoritative sources or are so altered as to have lost their authority."[40]

The Verity Educate study listed some of its key criticisms of the Newton materials:[41]

- Multiple, easily-refuted instances of inaccurate and false information

- Academic dishonesty ranging from plagiarism to deceptive editing

- Material taken directly from a hate-filled, religious, proselytizing website

- Assignments designed to prejudice students towards a radical position of a one-state scenario in Israel/the West Bank/Gaza

- Neo-Orientalist mistreatment of Arab perspectives

- Repeated biases against Israel and the U.S., and biases that sanitize the ideology and actions of terrorists

PENS provided copies of the Verity Educate report to school officials involved with the curriculum.[42] According to PENS, a follow-up meeting with those officials did not go well. The chair of the history department said he had no intention of reading the report and an assistant superintendent responded that she "was not allowed to read it, because she could only perform acts authorized by the School Committee." The Newton North High School principal instructed PENS representatives to bring their concerns to the Newton School Committee.[43] Verity Educate Executive Director Ellen Wald told a reporter from the Jewish News Service (JNS) that she approached Newton school officials three times with the report but did not receive a response.[44] As far as is known, the comprehensive Verity Educate report was not reviewed by Newton school faculty or the school committee.

Freedom of Information Act Request

The ad-hoc group and APT, now working together, demanded that the school system provide them with all relevant curriculum materials to ensure a complete review. (See Attachment 9.) One member of the group, Russel Pergament, who had published a local newspaper, *The Newton Tab,* later recalled his frustration with the school officials: "They were evasive and argumentative, and that compelled us to file a FOIA."[45] (See Attachment 10.)

In late 2014, the group turned to Citizens for National Security (CFNS), a Florida-based organization that had successfully exposed biased educational materials in Florida schools and had them removed.[46] CFNS, in turn, asked Judicial Watch,[47] a national group based in Washington, D.C., to file a Freedom of Information Act (FOIA) request with the Newton school system in order to gain access to the curriculum materials.[48]

According to CFNS Executive Director William Saxton,[49] the Newton schools began to comply with the FOIA request in May and June 2015,[50] providing materials from the 9th grade World History unit on Islam and the 10th grade unit on the Israeli-Palestinian conflict.[51]

Meanwhile, APT and the ad-hoc group, led by an energetic 93-year-old Newton resident Margot Einstein, continued with their efforts to publicize what they alleged were problems in the Newton curriculum. On April 7, 2016, APT screened a film *Indoctrination@Newton*[52] that provided a detailed exposé of the activities of Harvard's Center for Middle Eastern Studies Outreach Center and alleged that its influence on Newton educators was more extensive than Newton school officials admitted.

1   Denebola (Newton South High School newspaper), "Superintendent Responds to Parent Concerns About Middle East Curriculum," Dec. 8, 2012.

2   Its presence in the Center's curriculum was noted by Sandra Stotsky, *The Stealth Curriculum: Manipulating America's History Teachers,* Thomas B. Fordham Foundation, 2006, p. 31.

3   An interview with Tony Pagliuso conducted by Jack Morrissey of Christian and Jews United for Israel, available on Youtube. https://www.youtube.com/watch?v=j548BWo6x0c

4   *Indoctrination@Newton,* film by Americans for Peace and Tolerance. https://www.youtube.com/watch?v=JpSP0InxZYo

5   Wicked Local.com, "Parent: Newton South Material Defames Israeli Forces," October 7, 2011.

6   Interview with Margot Einstein, a Newton resident who organized this group, August 9, 2016.

7   Materials provided to the ad-hoc group included at least two articles identified as copied from the Arab World Studies Notebook. The second article, "An Introduction to Islam," was a basic discussion of central elements of Islam.

8   Statement by Superintendant David Fleishman at school committee meeting in October, 2012.

9   Newton Public Schools: *History Curriculum Statement,* undated. http://www.newton.k12.ma.us/cms/lib8/MA01907692/Centricity/Domain/506/History Curriculum Statement.pdf

10   www.JNS.org "Anti-Israel text remained in schools longer than officials let on, research shows," June 13, 2014. Also see: *Indoctrination@Newton* film by Americans for Peace and Tolerance.

11   Newton Public Schools: *History Curriculum Statement,* op. cit.

12   Video of school committee meetings available at www.newtontv.org.

13   *Propaganda, Proselytizing and Public Education: A Critique of the Arab World Studies Notebook,* American Jewish Committee, 2005.

14   Parents for Excellence in Newton Schools website, *Meeting with Deputy Superintendent for Teaching and Learning Ann Frederick – July 2012,* http://www.newtonparents.org/meeting-with-deputy-superintendent-ann-koufman-frederick.

15   Interview with Hillel Stavis, July 2016.

16   *The Jewish Advocate,* "Watchdogging Newton schools," August 10, 2012.

17   From notes made available to Steven Stotsky by Margot Einstein, founding member of the ad-hoc group.

18   Tapes of School Committee meetings are available on www.newtv.org; see especially meetings on October 24, 2011; November 14, 2011; April 9, 2012; April 23, 2012; May 14, 2012; June 11, 2012; November 15, 2012; and February 10, 2014).

19   *Newton Tab,* Nov. 14, 2012. Among other points, Hills claimed critics had not read the book they were complaining about (*A Muslim Primer*).

20   Parents for Excellence in Newton Schools (PENS). www.newtonparents.org/why-won-t-newton-schools-release-class-material

21   From notes made available to Steven Stotsky by Margot Einstein, founding member of the ad-hoc group.

22   A copy of the letter from Joel Stembridge, dated May 15, 2012 was provided to CAMERA.

23   A copy of this email is shown in the film *Indoctrination@Newton* by Americans for Peace and Tolerance (APT).

24   Parents for Excellence in Newton Schools website is viewable on-line.

25   Parents for Excellence in Newton Schools website, *Meeting with Deputy Superintendent for Teaching and Learning Ann Frederick – July 2012.* http://www.newtonparents.org/meeting-with-deputy-superintendent-ann-koufman-frederick

26   Ibid.

27   Americans for Peace and Tolerance is a Boston-based non-profit organization co-founded in 2008 by Charles Jacobs. It describes itself as "dedicated to promoting peaceful coexistence in an ethnically diverse America by educating the American public about the need for a moderate political leadership that supports tolerance and core American values in communities across the nation." It has produced a series of films exposing college campus anti-Israel bullying and an anti-Israel high school program. http://www.peaceandtolerance.org/

28   *Metro Boston,* October 23, 2013, "What are Newton students really learning?"

29   An ADL Report on the controversy is available on the PENS website http://www.newtonparents.org/adl-report

30   The Anti-Defamation League, Combined Jewish Philanthropies and Jewish Community Relations Council issued the following joint statement on Nov. 6, 2013:

"We appreciate that many people have been concerned about a recent ad that appeared in the Newton Tab, the Jewish Advocate, and the Boston Herald alleging that a biased anti-Israel curriculum has been integrated into classes and programs in Newton Public Schools. Based on a careful review of the materials at issue by ADL and JCRC, there is substantial reason to believe that the allegations made in the ad are without merit. The ad misinterprets certain elements of the materials and lacks reasonable context. The Newton School Committee and its leadership have been responsive, and have addressed the questions posed to them in a thoughtful, constructive way. In contrast, the ad's sponsor declined our invitation to explain the allegations and answer questions about them, a decision that we regret. We trust that this is reassuring to members of our community and that claims made against members of the Newton School Committee can now be put to rest. Israel faces many challenges. It is time for us to work together to meet them in a climate of respect and open discourse."

31   http://newengland.adl.org/files/2013/12/APT-Ad-12-30-13-2-docx-2.pdf.

32   *Boston Globe,* "*State Affirms School Curriculum After Protests*" Nov. 7, 2013.

33   Ibid.

34   *What Americans for Peace and Tolerance's (APT) Ad Alleges,* a response by the Anti-Defamation League to the allegations made by APT, Dec. 2013.

35   The ADL also joined with APT in condemning another secondary school program called Axis of Hope, developed by Carl Hobert under the auspices of Boston University. APT's film, "Axis of Bias" exposes the efforts at indoctrination in Axis of Hope. The ADL's Robert Trestan published a letter in the *Jewish Advocate* on July 3, 2015 sharply critical of Hobert's program and its defenders.

36   The PENS website offers a brief description of Flashpoints at http://www.newtonparents.org/flashpoints
A detailed examination is included in the Verity Educate report.

37   *The Jewish Advocate,* Letter to the Editor, Feb. 14, 2014, from Executive Director Jeremy Burton and President Jill Goldenberg, JCRC of Greater Boston.

38   Ibid.

39   Verity Educate, "Middle East Curricula in Newton Public Schools," September 2, 2014.
http://www.verityeducate.org/Newton/

40   PENS website, Executive Summary, Sept. 5, 2014. http://www.newtonparents.org/verity-educate-report
The Verity Educate study can be obtained by writing to Verity Educate for a copy. www.verityeducate.org/newton/

41   The Verity Educate summary of its findings, http://www.verityeducate.org/newton/

42   PENS website, "Meeting with Assistant Superintendent of Teaching and Learning Cynthia Bergen et al. –
December 2014," http://www.newtonparents.org/meeting-with-nps-administrators---december-2014

43   Ibid.

44   Jewish News Service, Sept. 19, 2014 http://www.jns.org/latest-articles/2014/9/19/as-report-elucidates-fracas-
on-anti-israel-texts-boston-area-school-district-remains-silent - Vwp6EkdLWSc=

45   Correspondence with Russel Pergament, August 2016.

46   Citizens for National Security (CFNS) identifies itself as a nonprofit, nonpartisan, public charity that identifies and
addresses threats to the United States from radical Islam, other extremist ideologies and rogue nations. It specializes
in research and education that provide ordinary citizens and public officials with accurate and credible information they
need to understand and act upon national security issues. https://cfns.us/

47   Judicial Watch identifies itself as a conservative, non-partisan educational foundation, that promotes transparency,
accountability and integrity in government, politics and the law. It advocates high standards of ethics and morality in
our nation's public life and seeks to ensure that political and judicial officials do not abuse the powers entrusted to
them by the American people. Judicial Watch fulfills its educational mission through litigation, investigations, and public
outreach. https://www.judicialwatch.org/about/

48   The MPRL request was sent to Superintendent David Fleishman on October 31, 2014.

49   FOIA materials released by the Newton schools.

50   Conversation with William Saxton, Chairman of CFNS, July 27, 2016

51   Correspondence by email with William Saxton on September 16, 2016. Newton schools indicated that both Newton
North High School and Newton South High School included a unit on Islam in the 9th grade World History course, but
only Newton South High School included a unit on the Israeli-Palestinian conflict in the 10th grade World History course.

52   One of a series of films on anti-Zionism and Islamic extremism by APT filmmakers Avi Goldwasser and Ilya
Feoktistov, http://www.peaceandtolerance.org/newton/

Part 3: Curriculum Analysis

The following analysis covers classroom materials provided by the school system in June 2015, as well as relevant items collected in 2011-2014. Some materials not currently in use were included because they could be in use by other school systems or could be reintroduced into the Newton curriculum. The Newton school system was asked for all materials relating to teaching about the Middle East, Islam and the Israeli-Palestinian conflict. Most of the materials provided pertained to the 9th and 10th grade World History courses. These materials included online videos, maps, handouts, and textbook chapters.

Many of the materials obtained in 2011-2014 were thoroughly evaluated by the Verity Educate study, as well as by prior CAMERA reports. The analysis that follows discusses only those materials deemed to be most important and relevant to conveying the Israeli-Palestinian conflict, Islamic history, and key issues in contemporary Islamic society.

The materials used in the unit covering the Israeli-Palestinian conflict consisted primarily of items found on the Internet. They provide only a partial view of the conflict, ignoring or downplaying many of the contributing factors. For example, largely concealed from the students are the religious component of the conflict, the persistence and extent of Palestinian terrorism, the oft-stated refusal by Palestinian leaders to accept a Jewish state, as well as the hate-filled rhetoric and incitement against Israel and Jews that saturates Palestinian political discourse. As a result, students are given a distorted view of the conflict and a misleading, benign image of Palestinian national movements. Former leader Yasir Arafat and current leader Mahmoud Abbas, are depicted as firmly committed to negotiating peace, when, in fact, many of their statements and actions suggest otherwise.[1]

The documents pertaining to Islamic history and culture expose students to varied perspectives on the establishment and expansion of Islamic rule. While some of the materials are sound, others are overly simplistic, emphasizing relatively moderate aspects of the Muslim conquests, while neglecting to amplify the discriminatory and repressive measures imposed on religious minorities. Supplemental materials are particularly problematic, often lacking factual substance and exhibiting a tendency to avoid critical scrutiny of Islamic society while unfairly tarnishing Americans as bigoted toward Muslims. Since the teachers of each class tailor their own syllabi, no two classes used identical materials.

Terrorism and radicalism in contemporary Islam are described as a deviation from traditional Islamic values and the result of misinterpretation by certain Muslims of key religious precepts like *jihad*. But there is no discussion of why Islamic radicals claim their version of Islam is the most genuine and carry out their attacks in the name of Islam. The units shed no light on how these radicals have managed to attract a significant following.

Absent from the Newton materials is any discussion of the incitement to hatred of Jews and Israel that permeates Palestinian society and much of the Middle East. Depictions of Jews as criminals and corrupters are ubiquitous in Palestinian media, schools, mosques, and government pronouncements.[2]

Palestinian terrorism is presented as limited to an extreme fringe that is unrepresentative of the main currents of Palestinian society. In reality, opinion polling in both the West Bank and in the Gaza Strip consistently shows extensive public support for acts of violence against Israelis.[3] And Palestinian society extols terrorists as heros to be emulated: For example naming schools, streets, cultural events, sports tournaments, and public squares in their honor.

Palestinian Chairman Abbas, PA Television, September 16, 2015 (Palwatch)

Also absent are readings by reputable Israeli and American historians whose accounts sharply differ from the perspectives presented. The inclusion of all major, credible perspectives is crucial to teaching critical thinking and would distinguish the aim of the course from indoctrination. But students are not only denied exposure to some of the important scholarship on the topic, they are misled as to what constitutes mainstream and fringe perspectives on the conflict.[4]

A. 10th Grade World History Unit on the Palestinian-Israeli Conflict

Overview: This unit contains items included in the 2015 FOIA release:

1. Two videos explaining the conflict from Internet web sites, including a 35-minute *New York Times* video that provided the basis of two days of discussion,

2. Two timelines for the conflict; an eight-page timeline from PBS, and a two-page timeline that includes a fill-in-the-blanks exercise,

3. Three maps from Palestinian or pro-Palestinian sources,

4. A 16-page photocopied handout including 15 maps, giving a summary of the political positions of important current figures,

5. An article discussing a two-state solution published in the *New York Times* by David Makovsky, an analyst associated with a Washington-based Middle East think tank,

6. An interactive website dedicated to "Middle East Peace."

Analysis of the unit also covers two textbook chapters. One textbook appears to be in current use although it is not specifically mentioned in the course syllabus. (See Attachment 11.) A second textbook is the source of a 10-page account of the history of the conflict that was used for several years, but was not included in the 2015 FOIA materials. Several handouts used in prior years that were not included in the 2015 FOIA release are also examined.

The unit presents a one-sided view of the conflict, shifting blame onto Israel and downplaying Palestinian responsibility for the situation:

- It promotes the view that the Israeli-Palestinian conflict is a "conflict over land" and that "this is not inherently a religious conflict."[5] (See Attachment 12.)

- It portrays the Palestinians as the indigenous people of the land, while obscuring the Jewish historical connection.[6] In addition, the materials often describe the West Bank as "occupied" rather than "disputed" and Israeli settlements are characterized as "illegal," even though official U.S. policy does not deem the settlements illegal and their status remains a matter of interpretation under international law. [7]

- It depicts Palestinians as victims, with no accountability for their actions and decisions that contribute to their current predicament.[8]

- It portrays the Palestinian Authority as unequivocally pro-peace and eager for negotiation, while portraying Israel as intransigent.[9]

- It conceals terrorism and instigation of violence by those affiliated with the Palestinian Authority (PA) and the Fatah party. Former PLO leader Yasir Arafat is portrayed as a man of peace; his extensive involvement in terrorism is whitewashed.[10] Mahmoud Abbas, Arafat's successor, is airbrushed as an uncomplicated advocate of a peaceful resolution to the conflict without any mention of his and the PA's glorification of terrorism and violence.[11]

1. Two Videos Explaining the Conflict

a. Challenges in Defining an Israeli-Palestinian Border: A five-part, 35 minute, *New York Times* video produced by Joe Burgess, Stephen Farrell, Alan McLean, Sergio Pecanha and Archie Tse.

This video series, to which the class devotes two days of discussion, is built on the faulty and deceptive premise that the Arab-Israeli conflict is mainly perpetuated by the failure to establish a permanent border between the two sides along the 1949 Armistice lines. [12]

What the series ignores is the steadfast refusal by Arab and Palestinian leaders to accept a permanent Jewish state in the region within any borders. The video contributes to an anti-historical account that identifies Israel's capture of the West Bank and Gaza in 1967 as the basis for Palestinian grievances, when in fact, Fatah and the Palestine Liberation Organization were founded with the goal of dismantling Israel well before 1967; Fatah in 1959 and the PLO in 1964.

Screenshot from the video

Students are not informed that all Palestinian leaders – including Palestinian President Mahmoud Abbas, who is portrayed as a moderate – have repeatedly articulated their rejection of a Jewish state. Nor is there mention of the key fact that Israel has made numerous, far-reaching offers of peace that entailed creation of a Palestinian state. The Palestinians' repeated refusal of these offers is essential information for students.

Indicative of Palestinian rejection of any Jewish state is the fact that in August 2016, Abbas pursued a lawsuit against Great Britain over the Balfour Declaration on the grounds that it led to what the Palestinians call their "catastrophe," or *Naqba* in Arabic, referring to the establishment of the State of Israel and the Arab initiated war triggered by the United Nations Partition Plan calling for the creation of a Jewish State and an Arab State in the Palestine Mandate.[13]

By ignoring salient elements of the conflict, the video misleads students about the essence of the conflict. And by focusing solely on Palestinian stated "goals" and Israeli actions that impede them, the film fails to examine Palestinian actions that prevent peace.

b. *Crisis Guide: The Israel-Palestinian Conflict,* Chapter II: An interactive video produced by the Council on Foreign Relations.

This video presents a relatively balanced overview, describing the geography and history of the Israeli-Palestinian conflict. It clearly states essential facts about Israel's acceptance and Arab rejection of the UN partition resolution in 1947 and the Arab invasion in 1948. It also presents the events leading to the 1967 war factually. The video, however, contains a significant factual error in stating that the pre-1967 Israel comprised 20,000 square miles. The actual figure was 7,847. This mistake seems unintentional (the area equals approximately 20,000 square *kilometers*).[14] Such errors should be corrected by editors.

2. Timelines for the Conflict

a. Promises/POV (Acclaimed Points of View) *A History of the Israeli-Palestinian Conflict,* American Documentary Inc., Dec. 2001: Produced by the Council on Foreign Relations and obtained from the PBS website. (See Attachment 13.)

This eight-page timeline, used by the 10th grade class as an "introduction to the Israeli-Palestinian conflict," presents a skewed chronology concealing much of the terrorism directed against Israel since its founding. It includes numerous errors and omits substantial relevant information.[15] The timeline is configured to present in parallel both an Israeli and a Palestinian account without any attempt to assess their accuracy. The timeline was produced by Negar Katirai, an intern with the Council on Foreign Relations.[16] Katirai credits Mark LeVine, an advocate of the BDS movement who teaches at the University of California at Irvine, with helping her develop the timeline. LeVine publishes vituperative[17] articles about Israel and Zionism[18] in which he has contended that Israelis have an "addiction" to violence and suffer from "collective mental illness."[19]

The timeline glosses over Palestinian/Arab ideology that rejects Israel's right to exist. The single reason given for the Arab rejection of the U.N. General Assembly's 1947 resolution to create a Jewish and an Arab state is that the Arabs "considered the proposal unrepresentative of the demographic distribution of Jews and Arabs living in Palestine," not that they opposed the creation of a Jewish state of any size in the region. [20]

Students are also told that in 1948: "Fighting breaks out between the newly declared state of Israel and its Arab neighbors," not that the five surrounding Arab states declared war on and invaded the fledgling Jewish state.[21]

The timeline's misleading recitation of UN Resolution 194 includes only the portion stating that Palestinian refugees who wish to return to the homes they fled should be permitted to do so. The part of the resolution requiring those refugees to "live at peace with their neighbours,"[22] (widely understood to require returning Palestinians to accept the presence of Israelis and abide by Israeli governmental authority) is omitted. Nor is there mention that all the Arab states voted against the resolution. Furthermore, the resolution had no legal force in any case as a General Assembly measure (only Chapter Seven Security Council resolutions are legally binding).

The timeline intimates that Israel's preemptive strike started the Six Day War, but fails to mention Arab leaders' calls to annihilate Israel, the Egyptian blockade of Israel's Red Sea passage, and the build up of Egyptian troops along Israel's Sinai border.[23]

The charred remains of an Israeli bus, attacked by Palestinian terrorists in 1978 Coastal Road Massacre

The timeline omits most of the terrorism perpetrated against Israeli civilians and conceals the glorification of terrorists by Palestinian leaders. There is no mention of Arab terrorist attacks inside Israel prior to the 1990s. Missing from the account are the coastal road massacre in March 1978, in which 25 adults and 13 children were murdered, [24] and the Maalot massacre in May 1974, in which 105 children were taken hostage and 25 eventually killed.[25] Yasser Arafat is portrayed as a man of peace, his extensive involvement with terrorism whitewashed. Instead students are simply told that in 1988: "Palestinian leader Yasser Arafat condemns all forms of terrorism and recognizes the state of Israel."[26]

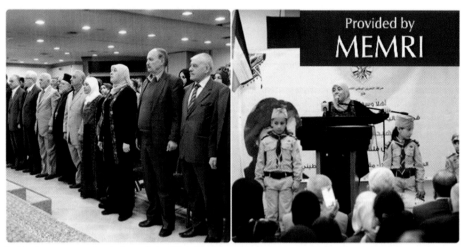

Public Commemoration in Ramallah of Dalal Mughrabi, who took part in the March 1978 Coastal Road Massacre, in which 38 Israeli bus travelers died, including 13 children

Disingenuously, the first terrorist act specified within Israel and the territories is the the rampage by a "militant Jewish settler" in 1994 that killed 29 Palestinians "praying at the main mosque in Hebron."[27] More recent Palestinian terrorism and the promotion of violence by affiliates of the Palestinian Authority and Fatah are likewise absent from the timeline.

The timeline is also out of date. It ends in 2001, and overly focuses on events in that and the preceding year. Students are deprived of information about Palestinian violence that reached its apex in 2002, when 452 Israelis were killed in terrorist attacks.

There is no mention of U.S. State Department-designated Palestinian terrorist groups, such as Al Aksa Martyrs brigades, Islamic Jihad, and the PFLP, or any of their attacks against Israeli civilians.

Palestinian gunman at the Munich Olympics in 1972

Although the timeline mentions the 1972 Munich massacre of Israeli Olympic athletes, it refers to the perpetrators from the Black September terrorist group simply as "gunmen."

The timeline mislabels the U.S. and E.U.-designated terrorist group Hamas as a "political group" although its own members reject the label of a political group, describing themselves as a "resistance movement."[28] As its charter makes clear and its leadership have repeated on many occasions, Hamas seeks to achieve its goals through violent means, not political.[29] There is no mention of the relentless rocket attacks by Hamas after the Islamist group seized control of Gaza in 2007.

Overall, the timeline suffers from shoddiness. For example, it claims Israel invaded Lebanon in 1982 to deal with attacks by Hezbollah, when, in fact, Hezbollah's hostilities with Israel began after the Israeli invasion.[30] The invasion was the culmination of years of conflict between PLO guerrillas in South Lebanon and Israel.[31]

b. Classroom timeline exercises

A classroom exercise requiring students to fill in the blanks on items in the timeline reveals a pattern of historical inaccuracy and omission similar to that of the POV timeline. For the year 1947, the classroom timeline notes that the "Arab Palestinians reject" the UN Partition Plan. This is inaccurate. The UN Partition Plan was rejected by the leaders of the existing Arab states and Palestinian Arab leadership, not by Arab Palestinians. [32]

Under the year 1972, it states "Palestinian *militants* (emphasis added) kill 11 Israeli athletes." The killing of the Israeli athletes was unambiguously a terrorist act, but is not identified as such.

Under the year 1993, the classroom exercise states, "Neither side denies the other's right to exist, and promise to work toward a final settlement." This is an example of creating false equivalence by failing to accurately convey the positions of each side. The Palestinians have never accepted the right of Israel to exist as a "Jewish" state.

c. *Middle East in Transition: Questions for U.S. Policy*, The Choices Program, Watson Institute for International Studies, Brown University. This 20-page chronogical account of the Arab-Israeli conflict was previously utilized. It contained numerous factual errors.

The bias is evident in the chapter's offering of harsh judgments of Israel and Zionists while ignoring the aggressive actions of Israel's adversaries. For example, the authors blame Israeli leaders for the Six-Day War and for "having little faith in diplomatic solutions," while the provocations by Arab leaders that prompted the war are concealed. The authors advance the discredited claim that the Israeli aerial attack on the U.S.S. Liberty was intentional.[33]

In describing the support for establishing a Jewish state in 1948, the authors present the offensive speculation that "Zionism might not have fulfilled its mission without the tragedy of the Holocaust." This deplorable canard suggesting that Zionists benefitted from the genocide against the Jews is a staple of anti-Israel and anti-Jewish agitators.

3. Maps of the Conflict

a. Maps from the Palestinian Academic Society for the Study of International Affairs (PASSIA).

Many of the maps used in the unit are informative. However, the maps disseminated by PASSIA, an organization that actively promotes the boycott and sanction movement, present a partisan narrative that justifies Arab actions and demonizes Jewish ones. For example, a map showing

Israel founded: Armistice
War broke out in 1948 when Britain withdrew, the Jews declared the state of Israel and troops from neighbouring Arab nations moved in. After 14 months of fighting an armistice line was created, establishing the West Bank and Gaza strip as distinct geographical units.

Palestinian Villages Depopulated in 1948 and 1967, and Razed by Israel

Palestinian Academic Society for the Study of International Affairs (PASSIA)

the 1949 Armistice line states "Jews declared the state of Israel and troops from neighboring Arab nations moved in."

Actually, the troops didn't simply "move in," they attacked Jewish communities.

A second map from PASSIA shows "Palestinian Villages Depopulated in 1948 and 1967 and Razed by Israel." Here PASSIA promotes the narrative of ethnic cleansing.[34] The scholarship on the issue reveals a more complex scenario of Arab flight, which was triggered by different stimuli at different points during the 1947-1949 conflict: Affluent Arabs left earliest, expecting to return after the fighting ended; some fled at the urging of their own leaders, reassured of their return after the Jews were defeated; many others fled in panic, frightened by stories of alleged Jewish atrocities spread by their own leadership; and others were driven from their homes as a result of battles between the two sides.

However, there are no maps in the curriculum showing the forced flight of Jews from Arab states. At the same time as the Palestinian Arab flight, a larger number of Jews fled from Arab states where they had lived for hundreds of years. Imperiled by the Arab-initiated war, the Jews were forced to abandon homes and livelihoods, arriving in Israel destitute. These Jews were largely absorbed by Israel.

b. Map of Israel and the territories since 1982 (unattributed).

A non-PASSIA map that ostensibly illustrates the borders of Israel from 1982 onward presents a partisan perspective. It refers to the West Bank and the Gaza Strip as "Palestinian territories occupied by Israel since the 1967 Six Day War."

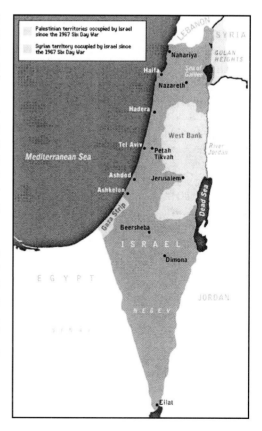

While there is considerable support for a "two-state solution" that would give the Palestinians much of the West Bank territory, United Nations Security Council Resolution 242,[35] which remains the basis of U.S. policy, did not identify these territories as Palestinian and left their disposition to be decided in negotiations of a final peace accord.[36]

The terminology also misleads because the territories that Israel captured in the 1967 war did not previously belong to the Palestinians; they were ruled by Jordan and Egypt. With regard to the Gaza Strip, in 2005 Israel withdrew from it, leaving the Palestinian Authority in charge of administering it. In 2007, Hamas seized control, ejecting the Fatah-dominated government.

4. "Understanding the Arab/Israeli Conflict"- (unattributed handout)

This 16-page handout drawn from multiple sources gives a summary of the political positions of the most important current figures in the conflict.[37] It handles Israel's founding reasonably well, but its treatment of more recent events and the current situation is flawed. It erroneously portrays the president of the Palestinian Authority as fully committed to negotiating a peaceful resolution of the conflict, while portraying the Israeli Prime Minister as resistant to negotiations.

The handout states, "President Mahmoud Abbas and the Palestinian Authority seek peaceful negotiation with Israel to establish a co-existing Palestinian state. The PA disagrees with Hamas' policy of armed struggle..."[38]

In fact, Abbas opposes two states for two peoples and has repeatedly said he will not accept a Jewish state. He has also chosen to bypass negotiations, seeking via the United Nations action to impose a settlement rather than meet with the Israeli government. In addition, Fatah, the political party which Abbas heads, affirmed its fealty to armed "resistance" in its general congress in 2009.[39]

The handout describes Israeli Prime Minister Benjamin Netanyahu and the Likud Party as "advocat[ing] for the continuation of Israeli settlements, continued Israeli control over the Palestinian territories, and the use of military pressure against Hamas." There is no indication of Netanyahu's freezing of settlement building and expressed willingness to meet with Palestinian President Abbas without preconditions. Nor does the description of Netanyahu's policy via Hamas provide accurate information or adequate context regarding the group's rocket and other attacks on Israel.

5. A Newspaper Article Discussing a Two-State Solution

In an opinion piece, "Mapping Middle East Peace," David Makovsky, Sept. 11, 2011,[40] a scholar at the Washington Institute for Near East Policy, asserts that a two-state solution is the only viable path to peace. Makovsky offers three scenarios of equal swaps of territory between Israel and a putative Palestinian state on the West Bank in order to bring Jewish West Bank settlers into Israel. The article is helpful in detailing the Jewish communities beyond the 1949 Armistice line (*The Green Line*), but it does not illuminate underlying political and religious forces that have stood in the way of what would otherwise be a relatively straightforward process of working out border adjustments.

6. Website of the S. Daniel Abraham Center for Middle East Peace

Students are advised to view the Center's website, which provides information on what are termed the core issues of the Israeli-Palestinian conflict, identified as: 1) Security, 2) Borders, 3) Jerusalem, 4) Refugees, and 5) Mutual Recognition.[41] The perspective presented reflects the positions of the Israeli and American left on reaching peace with the Palestinians.

The website is critical of Israeli Prime Minister Benjamin Netanyahu and accepts at face-value Arab representations of their willingness to live in peace with Israel in return for Israeli territorial concessions. This includes trust in the sincerity of the PLO declaration in 1988 that it no longer sought "all of Palestine" and was willing to accept just "22 percent" of Palestine (the West Bank and Gaza) and the desire of current Palestinian President Mahmoud Abbas to conclude a peace with Israel.

The website's list of events include reference to two meetings with Palestinian President Mahmoud Abbas but none with Israeli Prime Minister Netanyahu. The website provides several useful maps presenting different border proposals by the two sides based upon the principle of an equal swap of territories.

Textbook and Internet Readings on the History of the Conflict

1. *World History: The Human Odyssey*, Edited by Jackson J. Spielvogel, National Textbook Company, 1999.

Classes have utilized several textbooks that describe the Israeli/Arab wars and the emergence of the Palestinian refugee problem. These accounts downplay Arab refusal to accept Israel within any borders and promote the skewed notion of an equivalence of hardline sentiment on both sides with respect to accepting the other side. Similarly there is also a tendency to present the Zionist movement and Palestinian nationalism as parallel historical processes, when in reality Palestinian nationalism arose later and to a large extent as a reaction to the Jewish national movement.

This pattern of equating the sentiments and aspirations of both sides is evident in *World History: The Human Odyssey*. (Several chapters in the textbook discuss the Israeli-Palestinian conflict. The book remains in use in Newton schools, although it is not specifically listed in the 10th grade syllabus in the unit covering the Israeli-Palestinian conflict).

For example, in presenting the sentiments after the armistice of 1949, the book states: "The invasion failed, both sides remained bitter." [42]

In fact, the Israeli government immediately expressed interest in negotiating peace treaties, but the Arabs were adamant against any compromise.

This textbook also includes factual errors; for example, stating that the population of the Palestine Mandate after World War I was 98 percent Muslim. [43]

In fact, as many as 12 percent of the Arab population living in the Mandate at that time were Christian. In addition, the Jewish population numbered about 14 percent of the total population. [44]

The textbook misrepresents the Israeli position after the Six Day War, depicting Israel as unwilling to compromise and exonerating the Arabs. It states that Israel rebuffed Arab demands to return the territories taken in the war, offering the excuse that the acquired land improved their security. [45] But, in fact, in the immediate aftermath of the war, Israel did offer to turn over captured territories to the Arab states in exchange for peace and recognition of borders. In contrast the Arab states at their meeting in Khartoum, Sudan, in August 1967, issued what became known as the "three nos" – no recognition, no negotiations, no peace. [46] (See Attachment 14.)

2. *The Modern Middle East*, Chapter 14: "Origins of the Middle East Conflict," Oxford University Press, 3rd edition, 2011; 10-page account used from 2012-2013. [47] Also a five-page timeline from ***The Israeli-Palestinian Conflict*,** Cambridge University Press, 2010. Both are by James Gelvin. These readings were used in the 10th grade honors class at Newton South High School.

Gelvin's chapter and timeline were not among the materials released in 2015 - suggesting they may no longer be in use – but the themes he stressed[48] continue to be central to the Newton 10th grade unit on the Israeli-Palestinian conflict. Gelvin's chapter represents the most comprehensive example of the biased account imparted to Newton students. These themes and flaws were evident in an interview with a student who took the 10th grade course in 2016. [49]

Gelvin portrays the conflict as a war between Jewish colonialists who espouse what he alleges is a typical 19th century European nationalism – Zionism – against what he claims are the indigenous inhabitants, Palestinians. He misrepresents the history of the Jewish people, describing Zionism as "a nationalist movement that redefined a religious community – Jews – as a national community."[50]

In reality, Jews were defined as a nation from the outset, one that had lived dispersed in exile from its native land. He states as fact that "all [nationalisms] are defined by what they oppose… Zionism itself was also defined by its opposition to indigenous Palestinian inhabitants of the region."[51] This is inaccurate. Zionism is the national liberation movement of the Jewish people and from its inception, not a movement in opposition to others.

Nor did there exist a group of non-Jews who identified as "Palestinians" when the concept of Zionism was formulated.[52] At the time, "Palestinian" referred to the Jews of the area. Gelvin repeatedly uses the terms "Zionist" and "Palestinians," although contemporary documents routinely referred to the two sides as "Jews" and "Arabs." For example, he writes: the "British proposed dividing Palestine into two separate territories, one Zionist and one Palestinian." He describes the proposed partition as "between Zionist and Palestinian communities," [53] when in fact the British proposed to divide the Mandate into "Jewish" and "Arab" states.[54]

Gelvin reverses cause and effect concerning the "Arab intervention in 1948," writing that the "war that followed led to the creation of Israel." In fact, the war was launched after the U.N. supported the creation of the modern state of Israel in an effort to destroy it.

Gelvin retroactively applies current terminology to promote his hypothesis that "the dispute is, simply put, a real estate dispute"[55] involving "the confrontation between Zionist settlers and indigenous inhabitants."[56] The claim that the Palestinians are indigenous and that the Jews are outside settlers is likewise divorced from historical reality. [57]

Notably sidelined from Gelvin's account and missing entirely from his timeline, is Haj Amin al-Husseini, the Mufti of Jerusalem – whose office imparted both political and religious authority.[58] Husseini guided the Palestinian Arab national movement and shaped the political and religious content of its ideology. He injected an intolerant version of Islam, laden with anti-Jewish conspiracy theories into Palestinian dogma and fused it with fascist political ideology imported from Europe. He instigated Arab violence against the Jews in the 1920s, incited the uprising against the British in 1936, and was implicated in the assassinations of moderate Arab leaders in the Mandate.

Haj Amin al-Husseini and SS troops
Bundesarchiv-Koblenz, Collection: Yad Vashem

An admirer of European fascism, Husseini spent the WWII years in Berlin producing pro-Nazi propaganda and was instrumental in helping recruit several SS divisions of Bosnian Muslims. He pressed German leaders to expand their genocide against the Jews to the Middle East, even interceding to block a deal proposed by Nazi officials to exchange the lives of Jewish children for badly needed trucks. [59] After the war, he "escaped" Allied confinement in France and returned to the Middle East to organize violent opposition to the emerging Jewish state.

Husseini was not alone among Arab leaders in his extreme opposition to the Jewish state. Other prominent Arab leaders publicly exhorted fellow Arabs to wipe out the Jews.[60] These were not fringe zealots, but influential figures who set the direction for the Palestinian national movement, firmly affixing strictly interpreted religious doctrine to an already militant political ideology that opposed coexistence with a sovereign Jewish state.

Gelvin's "land-based" explanation for the conflict is shared by Harvard's Outreach Center and is echoed in the 10th grade World History course taught at Newton South High School. A Newton student who took the course in June 2016 recalled the teacher emphasizing to the students: "This is a conflict over land, not religion." [61] (See Attachment 15.)

What is obscured in the "land-based" account is that the territory is the Holy Land, sacred to Jews, Christians, and Muslims, and it is the latter, who view this conflict as a holy war, or *jihad*. Gelvin's minimizing of the religious aspect presents a serious problem because this component of the conflict has intensified, rather than diminished, over time. For example, in 1924, the Supreme Moslem Council published an English-language tourist guide to the Temple Mount acknowledging Judaism's historic bond to its ancient homeland and holy sites and the fact that the first and second temples stood on the Temple Mount.[62] Since the rise of the PLO and Yasir Arafat, Palestinian leaders have denied any Jewish connection to the Holy Land or the Temple Mount.

Because Gelvin does not acknowledge the importance of the religious component of the conflict, he cannot explain his observation that the conflict has attracted inordinate attention despite the fact that the "number of people directly affected by its political problems is miniscule in comparative terms" to other conflicts in the region and beyond.[63] By concealing the religious dimension of the conflict, he deprives students of the knowledge needed to understand the conflict.

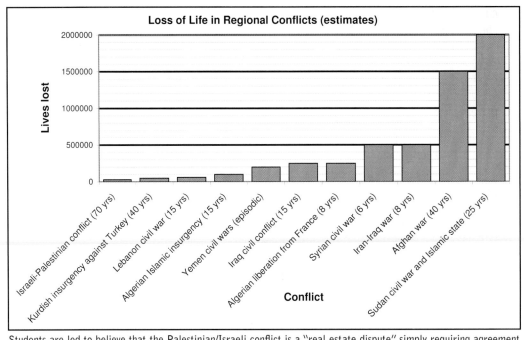

Loss of Life in Regional Conflicts (estimates)

Lives lost

- 2000000
- 1500000
- 1000000
- 500000
- 0

Conflicts (x-axis):
Israeli-Palestinian conflict (70 yrs), Kurdish insurgency against Turkey (40 yrs), Lebanon civil war (15 yrs), Algerian Islamic insurgency (15 yrs), Yemen civil wars (episodic), Iraq civil conflict (15 yrs), Algerian liberation from France (8 yrs), Syrian civil war (6 yrs), Iran-Iraq war (8 yrs), Afghan war (40 yrs), Sudan civil war and Islamic state (25 yrs)

Conflict

Students are led to believe that the Palestinian/Israeli conflict is a "real estate dispute" simply requiring agreement on borders. The religious component is de-emphasized. If the conflict is just a land conflict, like many others, then how are students to understand why the conflict is given such disproportionate attention and importance despite the much greater carnage of many other conflicts in the region?

A related, but separate issue is the false claim, starting with Haj Amin al-Husseini, that Jews were threatening Muslim holy sites on the Temple Mount. Husseini used the claim in 1929 to trigger deadly attacks in which more than one hundred Jews were murdered.

Synagogue desecrated by Arab rioters, Hebron

Scene of destruction in the Jewish Quarter of Hebron after the Arab riots of 1929

Since 1967, when all of Jerusalem and its holy sites came under Israeli control, this became the battle cry for violent *jihad*. Both the Palestinian Authority and Hamas have used false charges of threats to Islamic sites to inflame the passions of Palestinians and Muslims.[64] The Palestinian leadership continues to encourage violence in order to assert Muslim supremacy over Jerusalem's holy sites.[65]

Supplemental Material

1. Hamas Covenant

Students are given a radically altered one-page translation of the Hamas covenant that excludes all the passages revealing bigotry directed at Jews. In this way, Hamas's racial and religious supremacism is obscured and the Islamist group's agenda is portrayed as narrowly directed at political Zionism rather than the Jewish people.

Student handout translation of Article 28:

Jihad Against the Zionist Enemy: The Zionist invasion is a vicious attack that does not have piety... [and uses] all methods low and deplorable to fulfill its obligations... Zionists are behind the drug and alcohol trade because of their ability to facilitate the ease of control and expansion. The Arab countries surrounding Israel are requested to open their borders for the *Mujahideen* [Islamic fighters] of the Arab and Islamic countries so they can take their role and join their efforts with their Muslim brothers of Palestine. As for the other Arabic and Islamic countries, they are asked to ease the movement of *Mujahideen* from it and to it - that is the least they could do.

Full translation of Article 28:

The Zionist invasion is a vicious invasion. It does not refrain from resorting to all methods, using all evil and contemptible ways to achieve its end. It relies greatly in its infiltration and espionage operations on the secret organizations it gave rise to, such as the Freemasons, The Rotary and Lions clubs, and other sabotage groups. All these organizations, whether secret or open, work in the interest of Zionism and according to its instructions. They aim at undermining societies, destroying values, corrupting consciences, deteriorating character and annihilating Islam. It is behind the drug trade and alcoholism in all its kinds so as to facilitate its control and expansion.

Arab countries surrounding Israel are asked to open their borders before the fighters from among the Arab and Islamic nations so that they could consolidate their efforts with those of their Moslem brethren in Palestine.

As for the other Arab and Islamic countries, they are asked to facilitate the movement of the fighters from and to it, and this is the least thing they could do.

We should not forget to remind every Moslem that when the Jews conquered the Holy City in 1967, they stood on the threshold of the Aqsa Mosque and proclaimed that "Mohammed is dead, and his descendants are all women."

Israel, Judaism and Jews challenge Islam and the Moslem people. "May the cowards never sleep." [66]

The abridged student version edits out the most serious accusations that Jews corrupt society and are "annihilating Islam." Also, one section of the covenant describes the request for fighters from the surrounding Arab and Islamic states to join their "Muslim brothers of Palestine." But it omits the injunction, "We should not forget to remind every Moslem that when the Jews conquered the Holy City in 1967, they stood on the threshold of the Aqsa Mosque and proclaimed that 'Mohammed is dead, and his descendants are all women.' Israel, Judaism and Jews challenge Islam and the Moslem people. 'May the cowards never sleep.'"[67]

2. Prominent Voices on the One-State Solution and the Two-State Solution

A recurring problem of the class materials is the unwarranted attention given to fringe academics and activists. A two-page handout used in 2011-2013 titled "Prominent Voices on the One-State Solution and the Two-State Solution"[68] includes five anti-Israel agitators out of nine voices presented. The spectrum of voices runs from anti-Israel extremists to Israel's political left. Missing are the views of the majority of Israelis and of Palestinians in the West Bank. The skewed selection of voices misleads students into viewing fringe viewpoints as reasonable mainstream views.

The Verity Educate report observed, "This misleads students to believe that the mainstream position is a single state with a Palestinian majority when, in fact, this is a radical position."[69]

Prominent Voices include:

- John Spritzler, who runs a website advocating 9-11 conspiracy theories.[70]

- Virginia Tilley, an academic with no Middle East expertise and a supporter of the BDS movement.[71]

- Ali Abunimah, an apologist for Palestinian violence who co-founded and runs Electronic Intifada, an extreme anti-Israel website that promotes the BDS movement.[72]

- The late Professor Edward Said, a PLO adviser and opponent of the Oslo Peace Process.

- The late Professor Tony Judt, who denounced Zionism as irredeemably flawed and considered the Jewish state a historical mistake.[73]

- *The New York Times* columnist Thomas Friedman, caustic critic of Israeli policies and leaders. In December 2011, Friedman wrote, "I sure hope that Israel's prime minister, Benjamin Netanyahu, understands that the standing ovation he got in Congress this year was not for his politics. That ovation was bought and paid for by the Israel lobby."[74] Such a statement echoes anti-Semitic libels that Jews nefariously use financial means to advance their aims.

- Naomi Chazan, a former Israeli Knesset member whose views place her on the far-left edge of contemporary Israeli politics.

- Two Israeli Prime Ministers, one of whom, Ehud Olmert, raises the specter of a situation in Israel akin to South Africa, while the other, Shimon Peres, calls for a Palestinian state.

B. 9th Grade World History Unit on Islam

The 9th grade World History course covers Islamic history and culture. According to the Massachusetts standards on Islamic history formulated in 2002, students should understand significant aspects of Islamic belief, analyze the causes and effects of Islamic expansion and the achievements of the Islamic "Golden Age," and be able to describe the religious and political origins of conflicts between Islam and other religions, especially Christianity. [75]

The Newton materials include many of the important elements of these topics, but there is a marked tendency to downplay or gloss over negative aspects of Islamic history and societal practices. For example, the Massachusetts standards require students to learn about the importance of the slave trade in Islamic society. This topic is mentioned only in passing in a few textbook chapters, but is not dealt with substantively as the Massachusetts standards intended. Students are not informed, for example, that the Arab slave trade is estimated to have involved as many as 18 million black Africans, a number that is thought to be double in size to the slave trade to the Americas. [76] Nor are students informed that slavery, in its various forms was, until recently, still permitted in some Middle Eastern and North African societies.[77]

The FOIA release of material related to the 9th grade course encompassed 515 pages. Much of it was repetitious, as the material was divided up into separate sections for each individual class. Materials that did not deal with important historical events, cultural distinctions, or ideology – in other words, materials not prone to controversial interpretations or factual bias – were excluded from this analysis.

The materials examined below include:

- five readings from chapters from generalized world history textbooks,
- three selections from introductory textbooks on Islam,
- four newspaper or magazine articles,
- three photocopied handouts,
- classroom exercise,
- and one film.

The areas covered in the unit on Islam that are examined are

1. The status of women in Islamic societies,
2. Muslim doctrine,
3. The expansion of Islam, and
4. Bigotry against Muslims in the United States.

Also included in the analysis is an examination of a 32-page monograph used in an elective course on terrorism for 10th-12th graders.

Supplemental materials are chiefly used to present the status of women and anti-Muslim bigotry. These materials are factually weak.

Chapters from textbooks comprise the main source of information on the historic expansion of Islam and on religious doctrine. These tend to be factual, although problems still exist. Among those textbook selections included in the 2015 FOIA release are several that are reasonably balanced and informative. However, several textbooks demonstrate bias. One textbook, *World History: The Human Odyssey,* was criticized in the Verity Educate report for containing inaccuracies.[78] Holt, Rinehart, and Winston's *World History: Human Legacy* has also been criticized for inaccuracy and bias.[79] A third textbook, *World Civilizations: The Global Experience*'s further reading suggestions directing students to biased sources. [80, 81]

1. The Status of Women in Islam

a. *A Muslim Primer:Beginner's Guide to Islam*, by Ira Zepp, University of Arkansas Press, 2000. A 12-page chapter, "The Status of Women."

Some 9th grade classes have been assigned a chapter about the status of women in Islam from a book that purports to be a "primer" on Islam.[82] Written by Ira Zepp, who has no formal credentials in Islamic scholarship,[83] the chapter fails to offer a serious, dispassionate survey of women's conditions in Islamic culture. Instead it presents faulty and unproven assumptions about improvements over pre-Islamic society brought about by Islam.

The author offers unsubstantiated claims about the deplorable conditions of women in pre-Islamic society.[84] For example, Zepp favorably compares the attire of Muslim women to conceal their shape, hair and sometimes face, to the alleged attire worn by pre-Islamic Arabian women, whom he claims "were scantily attired and often topless;" and "as a result, they were abused by men."[85]

Zepp's assertion about women's wear in pre-Islamic Arabia is not supported by scholarship, including Islamic scholarship.[86]

Other unsubstantiated statements about the status of women in pre-Islamic society are his assertions that:

> "Two thirds of women in pre-Islamic society were slaves. They had no rights or legal and social status. Female infanticide was common. Men could have an unlimited number of wives...." [87]

Zepp includes dogmatic claims like "Islam and the Quran created major improvements in the status of women. They were oases in a desert of misogyny." [88]

In contrast to Zepp's portrayal of the improvements in women's status in Islamic society, the Muslim Women's League, an American Muslim organization whose mission is "to implement the values of Islam," wrote that:

> ...To claim that Arab women were universally inferior to men, and had absolutely no rights before Islam is too simplistic, and does not do justice to the women of this period...most of the information about the Arabian society before Islam is not uniformly accepted by all scholars in the field. In many cases, the factual information and evidence presented by some scholars have been refuted or contradicted by others...

Since the Arabs had no fully developed system of writing, the sources for this period are limited to traditions, legends, proverbs, and above all to poems.[89]

On the legal inequality of women under Islamic Shariah law, Zepp offers a broad societal rationale, explaining that the reason a women's testimony is valued at half that of a man's is because it "reflects a feeling that the women's emotional nature may prevent her from being as objective as a man."[90]

Zepp presents only positive aspects on women's status in Islamic societies, only briefly noting contrary perspectives and then rebutting them. He suggests that "we hear little about the diversity of women's opportunities in Islamic countries..." implying that Westerners fail to acknowledge "how many Muslim women are doctors, computer scientists, engineers, teachers, and bankers."[91] But he offers no further information to enable students to consider the validity of the claim.

In fact, women's rates of participation in the workforce vary widely among Islamic countries, but are considerably lower than in Western countries.[92] A study on gender inequality by the World Bank shows that Middle Eastern countries lag behind the rest of the world in various forms of legal protection for women.[93]

A more serious shortcoming is the author's concealment of information about practices like honor killings, genital mutilation, the stoning of women accused of adultery, or the treatment of women as property in some Islamic countries. Zepp could have chosen to argue that these practices are cultural artifacts distinct from or are distortions of Islamic teachings. But he chose instead to ignore the topic entirely.[94] It is crucial for students to see the entire picture of Islamic society and not just cherry-picked elements.

b. "In Depth: Civilization and Gender Relationships" [95] **"The First Global Civilization: The Rise and Spread of Islam,"** p. 136-137, from *World Civilizations: The Global Experience.*

This handout, consisting of two pages taken from a textbook, contradicts *A Muslim Primer* by contending that "women played active and highly valued roles in the bedouin tribes of pre-Islamic Arabia."

c. "Where Womanhood Reigns Supreme: The Seeds of My Own Re-evaluation," by Mary Walker (a personal account).

This two-page handout is an anecdotal account of an American woman who traveled to Africa to briefly live among Muslims and emerged from the experience convinced that women living in Islamic societies had more freedom than women in Western societies. The author, Mary Walker was a production coordinator for the BBC2 series "Living Islam." She describes her personal epiphany about Islam as she observed Muslim women first-hand over two years, as part of her job. She concludes, "The women had all exercised their right to choose. To some extent, they were freer than me. I had less control over my destiny. I could no longer point to them and say they were oppressed and I was not."[96]

This piece presents one perspective by a non-Muslim who was exposed for a relatively short period of time to Islamic society. It is an interesting perspective, but one that should have

Woman (left) wearing niqab, that covers hair and face, except for eyes

been presented in the context of various viewpoints that include both positive and negative perspectives of women raised in Islamic societies. Without learning about the grievances of those who criticize Islam's treatment of women, such as those of Ayaan Hirsi Ali, a Somali-Dutch Muslim who calls for reforming Islam, students are left with a narrow, one-sided view. Students also need to understand the grievances of Islam's critics in order to counter anti-Muslim arguments. The course should also include material that presents more rigorous and objective criteria, like the World Bank study on the status of women in Islamic societies.[97]

2. Muslim Doctrine

Basic elements of Muslim practice are conveyed to the students, such as the "Five Pillars of Islam."[98] The problems lie in the superficial treatment of controversial issues of contemporary importance, such as *jihad*. There is also a tendency to elevate Islam over Christianity and Judaism (as explained below).

For example, the syllabi of several sections on monotheism in the 9th grade unit indicate that more class days were devoted to the Muslim religion than to either Christianity or Judaism. Several students interviewed for this monograph questioned why so much time was allotted to Islam in light of the fact that Muslims comprise such a small portion of the U.S. population (slightly over 1 percent according to surveys in recent years).

a. Superficial Treatment of Jihad

i) "Islam: An Introduction," Saudi Aramco World, January/February 2002.

This three-page handout explains *jihad* as follows:

> The Arabic word *jihad* means "to struggle or strive, to exert oneself" for a praiseworthy aim. The "greater struggle" is a personal one: the struggle to resist temptation.... The "lesser struggle" is exertion for the sake of Islam, such as

working for the betterment of Muslim society or trying to persuade non-believers, by tongue or pen or by example, to embrace Islam. The lesser struggle may also include physical combat for the sake of Islam ... especially in self-defense and if carried out according to the explicit limitations imposed by the Qur'an. Some modern thinkers liken *jihad* to the Christian concept of a "just war."[99]

ii) Unattributed one-page handout discussing *jihad*

Another handout stated that "all Muslim scholars agree on the fact that the first, greatest *jihad* is the personal-spirited struggle towards discipline."[100]

While many Muslim sources directed toward Western audiences emphasize the non-warring meanings of *jihad,* many scholars express skepticism over the prominence of this interpretation for most Muslims. For example, Princeton University Emeritus Professor of Near Eastern Studies Bernard Lewis, a renowned expert on the history of Islam, offers a different definition of *jihad,* contending that it was used traditionally to rally Muslims to war against non-believers and that its object was to "bring the whole world under Islamic law."[101]

Muslim scholar Khaleel Mohammed, a professor of religious studies at the University of San Diego, stressed the importance of understanding that over the course of Islam's history, the main emphasis of *jihad* has shifted between the inner struggle to the obligation to war in the name of Islam. He stated, "Islam knows its share of violence, and to deny that history is disingenuous."[102]

b. Elevation of Islam Over Judeo-Christian Beliefs

i) *Islam, the Straight Path*, by John Esposito, Oxford University Press, 2010.

The five-page reading selection from a textbook, while informative, explains Muslim religious doctrine by relaying Muslim opinion about the falsity of Christian and Jewish beliefs. At points, the prose fails to make clear that this is Muslim *opinion* and not non-sectarian statements of fact. For example, the author writes, "After the falsification of the revelation given to the Jews and the Christians, God in his mercy sent down His word one final time."

The text contains no qualifier to clarify that this is what Muslims believe, nor does it include quotes to indicate that the author is quoting someone else's words. Rather, the author states this in his own voice.[103]

Further on he states, "Arabic is the sacred language of Islam because, in a very real sense, it is the language of God,"[104] again without any qualifier to indicate that this is a Muslim belief.

Esposito continues,

> "In contrast to Judaism and Christianity, whose Scriptures were not only translated into Greek and Latin at an early date but also disseminated in vernacular languages, in Islam Arabic has remained the language of the Quran and of religious learning."[105]

This is a misleading characterization of Jewish studies. While translations of the Jewish scriptures are available, religious scholars study Jewish scripture in its original Hebrew, which is also the primary language of study at Jewish schools and seminaries.

The use of Esposito's text also reflects a pattern of excessive reliance on academics who are anti-Western and anti-Israel. This raises concern that the materials may be tainted by their politics. For example, Stephen Schwartz, Executive Director of the Center for Islamic Pluralism, exposed Esposito's associations with numerous organizations that Schwartz identifies as "rife with anti-American, anti-Israel, and pro-Islamist propaganda camouflaged as scholarship."[106]

ii) "The Hajj: One American's Pilgrimage to Mecca," ABC News, *Nightline*, April 18, 1997. 22 minutes and 39 second video.

The narrator of the *Nightline* segment, Michael Wolfe, is an American of Jewish and Christian parentage who converted to Islam. He describes, in a reverential tone, his experience of doing the pilgrimage to Mecca, a religious duty of all Muslims. In the segment, *Nightline* host Ted Koppel erroneously states that there are "more than 5 million Muslims" in the United States, "more American Muslims than Jews." In fact, credible counts found between 2-3 million Muslims in the U.S., less than half the Jewish population. Wolfe also betrays a negative attitude toward Christianity and Judaism, stating, "I find the absence of priests and rabbis attractive" and he claims that non-Muslims are excluded from Mecca to "preserve its sanctity and protect pilgrims."[107]

iii) Classroom exercises on Islam

Some 9th grade Newton World History classes include an exercise in which students are asked to memorize lines from the Quran. Students are also assigned a project to write about Islamic cities from the perspective of Muslim pilgrims carrying out the duty of the pilgrimage to Mecca (Hajj). Included among these cities is Jerusalem. Students are asked to "present an overview of your homeland" and prepare a city banner.

While such exercises may not represent overt indoctrination, they cause discomfort to many as entailing activities that seemingly cross the line into promoting religion in public schools.

3. Expansion of Islam

Students are provided brief excerpts from contrasting textbook accounts of Islam's expansion. Most classes present students with both positive and negative assessments of Muslim conquest and rule. However, class assignments and the phrasing of questions on tests emphasize a portrayal of Muslim conquerors as tolerant toward their conquered subjects, without offering solid factual evidence to back up such a sweeping and questionable assessment.

a. Class Assignment - How Should Early Muslim Armies Be Remembered?

a) A two-paragraph excerpt from the 1999 textbook *World History: Connections Today* states that the Muslims were "in general decent conquerors" and that "many of the conquered regions welcomed the Arabs as liberators."[108] This account portrays the Arab conquerors as demanding only a "reasonable" tribute.

b) Another two-paragraph excerpt taken from an earlier, 1936 textbook, *A Little History of the World*, in contrast, portrays Arab warriors as wantonly destructive, killing or converting all non-believers.[109]

Without any further information about the scholarly quality of each source or additional evidence, students are asked to judge "which do you think is fairer? (i.e. more accurate)." How would students know which is fairer (or for that matter, if either account was credible) if both accounts are treated as equally valid? Students are then asked, "How should the early Muslim armies be remembered?"

b. Misportraying Forced Conversions as Voluntary

Several handouts and textbook accounts present Muslim conquests as unusually tolerant and contend that conquered subjects were so impressed with Islam that many voluntarily converted.

i) For example, a handout labeled **"DBQ6, Spread of Islamic Civilization"** includes a reading assignment labeled **"Document B: Verses from the Qur'an"** that contends that conquered subjects converted voluntarily:

> "It is often incorrectly assumed that Islam spread so quickly because Muslims forced people to convert. Although this sometimes happened, the Quran forbids the practice especially in regards to the People of the Book. When People of the Book came under Muslim rule, they could choose to convert voluntarily, or they could pay a tax called jizya. If they chose to maintain their religion and pay the jizyah, they were granted certain religious and political rights and privileges."[110]

ii) One textbook, *World Civilizations*, **Chapter 6: The First Global Civilization: The Rise and Spread of Islam**, p. 138, offers an account of the Muslim conquests in which, "Most converts were won over peacefully through the great appeal of Islamic beliefs and advantages they enjoyed over non-Muslim peoples in the Empire."[111]

iii) An unattributed handout titled, **"Spread of Islam Cause and Effect"** ascribes the successful expansion of Islam to "Easy acceptance of the social ideas of Islam, equity [equality?] among believers"[112] and contends that "[they were] good warriors – not afraid to die." The handout concludes that "In general, [they were] decent conquerors (easier on some than their previous rulers had been)" who offered conquered people three choices: "convert to Islam", "pay a reasonable tax" or "die." It asserts that Jews and Christians were treated with "much respect."

iv) Another textbook, *Early Islam,* posits that minorities were treated with "much more tolerance" than under previous rulers and asserts that Muslims were "especially liberal with the Jews and Christians."[113]

The characterizations by all these sources of the conditions of religious minorities under Islam are misleadingly rosy. While historical accounts provide examples of Islamic rulers extending a degree of tolerance toward non-Muslims that was unusual for the time, there was never any question about the inferior status of non-Muslims.

Early Islam author Desmond Stuart's use of the term *liberal* connotes equal rights and opportunities free from discrimination as applied in contemporary parlance. This is inappropriate terminology to represent even a relatively tolerant portrayal of the lot of religious minorities under Muslim rule. The terminology obscures the fact that the *jizya* was a coercive tax and those who chose not to convert faced legal discrimination and inferior social status. Students are misled about the rights and social status of non-Muslim minorities (*dhimmis*) under Islamic rule. Jews and Christians did not enjoy equal rights to Muslims, had to pay substantial protection taxes, and lived as stigmatized subjects in tenuous and at times dire conditions.

As historian Efraim Karsh of the University of London noted, non-Muslims

> "suffered from social indignities and at times open persecution. Their religious activities outside the churches and synagogues were curtailed, the ringing of bells forbidden, the construction of new church buildings prohibited and the proselytizing of Muslims was made a captial offense punishable by death. Jews and Christians had to wear distinctive clothes to distinguish them from their Muslim lords, could only ride donkeys, not horses, could not marry Muslim women, had to vacate their seats whenever Muslims wanted to sit..."[114]

Concerning conversion, the texts offer no substantiation of their assertions that an important factor in conversion was the appeal of Islam as opposed to factors like self-interest or coercion. Such conjecture smacks of indoctrination and is unscholarly. More scholarly treatments of the early history of Islamic expansion describe a slower and different process of conversion.

According to Karsh,

> "Arab conquerors were far less interested in the mass conversion of vanquished peoples than in securing tribute. Not until the second and third Islamic centuries did the bulk of these populations embrace the religion of their latest imperial masters, and even this process emanated from below in an attempt to escape paying tribute and to remove social barriers, with the conquering ruling classes doing their utmost to slow it down."[115]

There are also significant omissions in the discussion of Islam's treatment of conquered groups. For example, none of the sources reviewed mention the story alleging that hundreds of members of the Jewish Meccan tribe, the Qurayza, were beheaded in 627 AD for rejecting Muhammad as the Prophet.

4. Bigotry Against Muslims in the United States

Students are presented with a negative image of an America infected by rampant Islamophobia. Sensationalized and controversial articles with little factual substance portray Americans as bigoted against Muslims. There is no attempt to bring balance by presenting Americans who do not consider their concerns about the actions perpetrated by radicalized Muslims in the name of Islam as unwarranted and bigoted. In addition, there is no effort to compare anti-Muslim bias to bias against other religious groups. For example, according to annual FBI statistics, Jews are by far the most frequent targets of religiously-based hate crimes in America. (In 2015, the FBI reported 664 anti-Jewish incidents with 731 victims and 257 anti-Muslim incidents with 307 victims).[116]

a. "Islamophobia: Does America Have a Muslim Problem," Bobby Ghosh, *Time Magazine,* Aug. 30, 2010. [117]

This controversial five-page opinion piece by the then-world editor of *Time Magazine* levels the irresponsible and unproven charge that Americans are inherently racist against Muslims. The author states without any basis that "Islamophobia has become the accepted form of racism in America" and "You can always take a potshot at Muslims or Arabs and get away with it." [118]

Time article

The piece is sloppy and unresearched, based solely on opinion. It includes allegations that are contradicted by the preponderance of evidence. For example, Ghosh claims, despite FBI statistics to the contrary, that "Jews, Mormons and others still experience hate speech. But the most toxic bile is reserved for Muslims."

Furthermore, recent exposure of a wave of anti-Semitism sweeping college campuses, often driven by Muslim organizations and the anti-Israel organization Students for Justice in Palestine, indicates that the bulk of hate speech on campus is against Jews, contrary to the article's implication. [119]

The article is also inappropriately political, alleging Republican politicians, like former President George Bush, Sara Palin and Newt Gingrich, stoked anti-Muslim prejudice. While such posturing may be acceptable in a magazine op-ed, it has no place in a classroom that is ostensibly teaching facts.

b. "Disney sued for discrimination by former employee over Muslim hijab," *Guardian,* Aug. 14, 2012; [120] and

c. "Islamic emblem of bias also trigger for bias," *The New York Times,* Nov. 3, 1997. [121]

Students were given these two newspaper feature stories on Muslim women who insisted on wearing their *hijab* and sued alleging discrimination when they were told they could not wear it. While a legitimate topic, it is too narrowly presented when limited to Muslims. This imparts the inaccurate message that such issues are solely a matter of bigotry directed against Muslims. It should be framed as part of the larger debate over the limits of public religious displays, including skullcaps, turbans, kirbets, and other religious identifiers. It also belongs in a debate about customs that may raise concerns about public safety. The *Guardian* story is too simplistic, conveying the sense that those objecting to a fellow employee wearing the hijab are simply motivated by irrational feelings. The article also incorrectly sets the American Muslim population at six million.

In sum, many Newton assignments treat aspects of the history of Islam, its doctrine, and the customs of Islamic culture with such caution and disregard for factual information that they fail to educate students adequately or to promote critical thinking skills. As a consequence, the unit on Islam, at points, takes on the characteristic of indoctrination rather than dispassionate historical survey.

C. Terrorism Elective

Responding to Terrorism: Challenges for Democracy, The Choices Program, Watson Institute for International Studies and Brown University.

The 32-page monograph's first example of terrorism is the seizure by Palestinian terrorists from the Black September group of Israeli athletes at the 1972 Munich Olympics. The monograph rationalizes the terror act by simply stating that the reasons given for the terrorist act were Israel's holding of Palestinian prisoners and Israeli "government policies."[122] The account states:

> "The public was shocked by images of the crisis and by the idea that the Israeli athletes, who were obviously not directly responsible for their government's policies, would be held accountable for those policies. The athletes were targeted simply because they were representatives of Israel – and, by extension, of Israel's policies."[123]

Students are not informed that the Palestinian prisoners held by Israel were convicted or suspected of involvement in terrorism and that the Munich terrorists tortured the Israeli victims.[124]

The reading provides four different examples of religiously motivated terrorism. The 1993 World Trade Center bombing by a group of Islamic radicals; the 1994 attack on Palestinian worshippers at a Hebron mosque by an Israeli individual, Baruch Goldstein; the sarin gas attack on the Tokyo subway system by members of a Japanese Buddhist cult; and the 1985 rampage in Arkansas by Richard Snell, adherent to the racist Christian Identity sect in the United States. The intent seems to be to demonstrate that terrorists can arise from diverse religious backgrounds. But there is an inherent distortion in this egalitarian approach, because it fails to convey the fact that contemporary terrorism is overwhelmingly the work of Islamic radicals, many of whom identify with extensive networks, while the Jewish and Buddhist acts were isolated incidents.

The monograph asserts that, "Most interpretations of Islamic tradition note a history of tolerance and peace."[125] But no evidence is presented to bolster this broad statement. For example, the monograph could have cited public opinion polls or statements by Muslim leaders condemning terrorism. Presenting such a sweeping claim as an undisputed statement without providing any evidence denies students the information necessary to refute contrary allegations. Other generalizations are similarly presented as self-evident fact without substantiation. For example, in discussing U.S. relations with Israel the monograph states that "America's attachment to Israel has attracted fresh attention. Israel's treatment of the Palestinians and its attacks against Hezbollah in Lebanon have drawn more intense criticism."[126] What aspect of "Israel's treatment of Palestinians" or "attacks against Hezbollah in Lebanon" deserves criticism? Who is doing the criticizing? This essential information is missing.

Summary of the Materials used in the 9th and 10th Grade and in the Elective Course

There are common threads connecting the Newton 10th grade unit teaching about the Israeli-Palestinian conflict and the 9th grade unit teaching about Islamic history and culture. In both cases handouts used to teach these topics emphasize the non-Western perspective, without critical examination. Rather than confronting controversial issues and providing students with sufficient background and arguments to counter stereotypes, these issues are downplayed or ignored.

Students are exposed to points of view that are not supported by evidence or based on fact. The 10th grade unit on the Israeli-Palestinian conflict revises history to present the current Palestinian predicament as primarily Israel's fault. The materials cast the Palestinians as the aggrieved victim lacking agency of their own. Missing from these accounts is the unwillingness of the Palestinian leadership (both more secular and Islamist) to accept the legitimacy of the Jewish state and to prepare its population for a lasting – as opposed to temporary - peace.

The 9th grade's account of Islam is flawed by an unwillingness to delve into the topic of Islamic radicalism. It fails to articulate how Islamic radicals borrow from Islamic doctrine to promote a totalitarian, misogynistic mass movement. The materials do not adequately explore the underlying causes of turmoil and dysfunction in many Islamic states and fail to explain the emergence of international terrorists who claim the mantle of Islam and are able to attract a substantial following.

Materials obtained in 2015 through the FOIA request did not include some of the most biased readings criticized in the 2014 Verity Educate report. Previously used but not in the 2015 FOIA release were chapters copied from an Internet website called Islamicweb.com, that according to Verity Educate, contained "numerous diatribes against Jews, Christians, Shi'a Muslims and other non-Sunni Muslims"[127] and "promote[d] hatred, violence and vitriol,... and perpetuate[d] numerous inaccuracies about Islam, other religions, and history."[128] It is possible that the publicity surrounding the use of controversial materials may have prompted some Newton educators to take greater care in selecting the materials they use in the classrooms. Two examples of more balanced materials are *Crisis Guide: Israeli-Palestinian Conflict* (Interactive) [129] and *Religions of the World*, Edited by Breuilly, O'Brien, Palmer. [130] In contrast to the omissions in the chapter by James Gelvin and in the POV timeline, the *Crisis Guide* interactive discloses Haj Amin al-Husseini's "alliance with Adolf Hitler."

Selections by reputable mainstream scholars, like Bernard Lewis, are missing. The exclusion of important and credible points of view raises valid concerns about the degree to which students are exposed to indoctrination rather than critical learning. Also nowhere to be found is the eloquent prose of Egyptian-born historian Fouad Ajami, whose articles appeared for decades in the American news media, and whose widely acclaimed book, *The Dream Palace of the Arabs*, makes ideal reading for high school students. These scholars, who are sympathetic to Islam, could provide crucial insight to students in understanding the environment of many Muslim-dominant societies. Instead, much of the material was produced by authors and videographers who lack expertise in the history and practice of Islam or the history of the Israeli-Palestinian conflict.

A further component of the teaching units involves the frequent reliance on student role-playing as an activity to debate the conflict. Students are instructed to argue a particular side and try to offer solutions to achieving peace. For such role-playing exercises to serve any useful purpose, students need all the relevant and accurate information. That includes informing students about unpleasant aspects of contemporary Palestinian culture that honors terrorists and inculcates Palestinian children with a favorable view of violence and hatred. Examples of this are readily available from MEMRI (Middle East Media Research Institute[131]) and PMW (Palestinian Media Watch[132]), two organizations that record and translate speeches, television programs, sermons, and textbooks in the Palestinian Authority, Gaza, and the Arab world.

Use of role-playing dependent on the skewed information conveyed in many of the materials will likely only intensify the misunderstanding of Middle East realities.

1   CAMERA, "Abbas Rewrites History," May 17, 2011, critique of Abbas op-ed in *The New York Times.*

2   MEMRI and Palestinian Media Watch are two organizations that document the rampant incitement to hatred that permeates Palestinian society and institutions.

3   E.g. *Washington Free Beacon,* Aug. 27, 2014. http://freebeacon.com/national-security/poll-89-percent-of-palestinians-support-terror-attacks-on-israel/

4   There are numerous historians who have published notable works of scholarship on the Israeli-Palestinian conflict whose views are not represented in the curriculum. For example, Efraim Karsh, author of *Palestine Betrayed,* offers a detailed account of the events that lead to Palestinian flight during 1947-49.

5   "Class Notes for Israel Palistine [sic] (Student and Teacher Discussion)," May 1, 2013. See attachment #12, p 90.

6   James Gelvin, *The Modern Middle East,* Chapter 14, "The Origins of the Israeli-Palestinian Dispute,"', Oxford University Press, Third edition, 2011.

7   A handout labeled "The Five Points of Peace: Debate Preparation" states, "it is recognized that these settlements [Jewish settlements in the West Bank] are illegal under international law."

8   As reported in an interview conducted by Steven Stotsky of Newton South High School sophomore, June 2016.

9   Class handout titled "What position does Mahmoud Abbas hold?"

10 As reported in an interview conducted by Steven Stotsky with Newton South High School sophomore, June 2016.

11 For example, the unit conceals the fact that the PA continues to pay salaries to Palestinians convicted of terror offenses and that the PA hails terrorists as heroes.

12 CAMERA review of New York Times video, "Challenges in Defining an Israeli-Palestinian Border," http://www.camera.org/index.asp?x_context=2&x_outlet=35&x_article=3417

13 http://www.haaretz.com/israel-news/.premium-1.733256

14 *Crisis Guide: The Israel-Palestinian Conflict,* Chapter II, Council on Foreign Relations. http://www.cfr.org/israel/crisis-guide-israeli-palestinian-conflict/p13850

15 Verity Educate, p. 35-46 provides a comprehensive review of the timeline, identifying numerous errors.

16 Negar Katirai, Promises/POV *A History of the Israeli-Palestinian Conflict,* American Documentary inc., Dec. 2001. http://pov-tc.pbs.org/pov/pdf/promiese/promises-timeline.pdf

17 *FrontPage Magazine,* "Mark LeVine unhinged on Facebook," Dec. 11, 2014. LeVine's intemperance toward Israel and anyone who supports it was evident in a profanity-laden outburst on Facebook in 2014: "Call me uncivil, but still fuck you. Fuck all of you who want to make arguments about civility and how Israel wants peace. There is only one criticism of Israel that is relevant: It is a state grown, funded, and feeding off the destruction of another people. It is not legitimate. It must be dismantled, the same way that the other racist, psychopathic states across the region must be dismantled. And everyone who enables it is morally complicit in its crimes, including you."

18 Mark LeVine, *Al Jazeera,* "The tide is turning against Zionist extremism" Oct. 20, 2015.

19 *Huffington Post,* Jan. 13, 2009.

20 POV timeline, p. 2.

21 Ibid, p. 2.

22 UN Resolution 194. http://www.israellawresourcecenter.org/unresolutions/fulltext/unresga194.html

23 POV timeline, p. 3.

24 *The New York Times,* March 11, 2010. Also see PMW. http://www.palwatch.org/main.aspx?fi=680&fld_id=680&doc_id=4695

25 A compendium of Palestinian terrorist attacks against Israelis can be found on the Jewish Virtual Library website: http://www.israellawresourcecenter.org/unresolutions/fulltext/unresga194.html

26 POV timeline, p. 4.

27 POV timeline, p. 5.

28 *Ma'an News Agency,* "Hamas leader concedes mistakes were made in 2006 rise to power in Gaza," September 25, 2016. https://www.maannews.com/Content.aspx?id=773287https://www.maannews.com/Content.aspx?id=773287

29 Verity Educate, p. 43.

30   Tony Badran, "The Secret History of Hezbollah," Nov. 18, 2013, Foundation for the Defense of Democracies. http://www.defenddemocracy.org/media-hit/the-secret-history-of-hezbollah/

31   *Israel and Lebanon: Problematic Proximity,* Rubin Center, IDC Herzliya, 2009. http://www.rubincenter.org/2009/06/spyer-2009-06-01/

32   Timeline fill-in-the-blanks exercise, unattributed handout.

33   Verity Educate provides a lengthy examination (p.124-152) of the Brown University booklet identifying numerous examples of errors and exposing the overall bias of the material.

34   Efraim Karsh, *Palestine Betrayed,* Yale University Press, 2010.

35   See attachment 1 for the wording of UNSC Resolution 242.

36   The following articles document the intent of the framers of the resolution and emphasize their careful wording of the resolution. http://www.discoverthenetworks.org/viewSubCategory.asp?id=603, http://www.camera.org/index.asp?x_context=2&x_outlet=118&x_article=1267.

37   An examination of the materials by Verity Educate identified the sources of the handout as the *Middle East and Islamic World Reader,* edited by Marvin E. Gettleman and Stuart Schaar, Grove Press.

38   Ibid.

39   CAMERA, "The Sixth Fatah Congress: The Myth of Moderation," Aug. 12, 2009.

40   David Makofsky, "Mapping Mid East Peace" *The New York Times,* Sept. 11, 2011.

41   S. Daniel Abraham Center for Middle East Peace. http://www.centerpeace.org/

42   Jackson J. Spielvogel, *World History: The Human Odyssey,* National Textbook Company, 1999. From Chapter 32: The Rise of Arab Nationalism and the Problem of Palestine, p. 1058.

43   Verity Educate, p. 101-108 provides a detailed examination of the Spielvogel text, identifying numerous errors in the historical account of Zionism and the Palestine Mandate.

44   Figures from Sergio DellaPergola, Demography in Israel/Palestine: Trends, Prospects, Policy Implications, August 2001.

45   Spielvogel, p. 1063.

46   The Six Day War, CAMERA, 2007, Khartoum resolution, http://www.sixdaywar.org/content/khartoum.asp

47   See *The Jewish Advocate,* "Learning some hard lessons about Newton's curriculum," by Charles Jacobs and Ilya Feoktistov, May 23, 2014.

48   James Gelvin, "The Origins of the Israeli-Palestinian Dispute."

49   As conducted in an interview by Steven Stotsky of a student who took the 10th grade course in June 2016. According to the student, the teacher emphasized to the class that this was a conflict over land, not religion.

50   Gelvin, p. 218.

51   Gelvin, p. 211.

52   According to Jewish Virtual Library, "the term Zionism was coined in 1890 by Nathan Birnbaum...
It is the national movement for the return of the Jewish people to their homeland and the resumption of Jewish sovereignty in the Land of Israel."

53   Gelvin, p. 212.

54   Andrea Levin, "Touching A Nerve – Palestinian Origins," http://www.camera.org/index.asp?x_context=55&x_article=2170

55   Gelvin, p. 206.

56   Ibid, p. 233.

57   For another critical review of Gelvin's text see Verity Educate's report, pages 95-101. The report identifies numerous examples where Gelvin misrepresents historical events and documents in order to support his biased history.

58   Steven Stotsky, "Review of *The Israel-Palestine Conflict: One Hundred Years of War,*" by James Gelvin, CAMERA, May 23, 2013.

59   For a detailed examination of Haj Amin al-Husseini's involvement with the Nazis, in particular his role in blocking the rescue of 1000 Jewish children, see Jennie Lebel's *The Mufti of Jerusalem: Haj-Amin el-Husseini and National-*

Socialism, published by Cigoja Stampa, Belgrade, Serbia, 2007.

60   Yoram Ettinger provides a synaopsis of these statements (from his E-mail posting on 5-27-2016): On October 11, 1947, Abdul Rahman Azzam Pasha, the first Secretary General of the Arab League told the Egyptian daily *Akhbar al Yom*: "…This will be a war of extermination and momentous massacre, which will be spoken of like the Tartar massacres, or the Crusaders' wars…. Each fighter deems death on behalf of Palestine as the shortest road to paradise….The war will be an opportunity for vast plunder…. " On August 2, 1948, the *NY Times* reported that the founder of the largest Islamic terror organization, the Muslim Brotherhood, Hassan al-Banna, instigated: "Drive the Jews into the sea… and never accept the Jewish State."

61   Interview by Steven Stotsky in July 2016 of a student who took the 10th grade course in June 2016.

62   *A Brief Guide to al-Haram al-Sharif - Temple Mount Guide Pamphlet,* by Supreme Muslim Council (1924), January 1, 1924. https://www.amazon.com/Brief-Guide-al-Haram-al-Sharif-Temple/dp/0971051178/ref=sr_1_cc_1?s=aps&ie=UTF8& qid=1468858286&sr=1-1-catcorr

63   Gelvin, p. 217.

64   Ricki Hollander-CAMERA, "Hamas and Fatah Working in Lockstep to Incite and Attack", November 6, 2014. http://www.camera.org/index.asp?x_context=7&x_issue=16&x_article=2868

65   CAMERA, "The Battle over Jerusalem and the Temple Mount," Nov. 6, 2014. http://www.camera.org/index. asp?x_context=55&x_article=1404http://www.camera.org/index.asp?x_context=55&x_article=1404

66   http://avalon.law.yale.edu/20th_century/hamas.asp

67   Verity Educate, p. 56.

68   Class handout, "Prominent Voices on the One State solution and the Two State Solution."

69   Verity Educate, p. 14-16 provides a detailed discussion of the 9 individuals featured in the handout.

70   John Spritzler, "Should there be a Jewish state?" *Axis of Logic,* April 13, 2004.

71   Virginia Tilley, "On the Academic Boycott of Israel," Electronic Intifada, May 27, 2007.

72   Electronic Intifada is a website that features radical positions. According to Verity Educate, "Entire sections of the website are devoted to activism on behalf of Palestinian militants… Abunimah… has made hateful statements such as that Zionism is a continuation of Nazism."

73   Tony Judt, "Israel the Alternative," *New York Review of Books,* Oct. 23, 2003.

74   *The New York Times,* Dec. 14, 2011.

75   Reproduced in the *Stealth Curriculum, Manipulating America's History Teachers,* Sandra Stotsky, Thomas B. Fordham Foundation, 2006, Appendix A.

76   *Ballandalus, Crescat scientia vita excolatur,* Trans-Saharan Slave Trade and Racism in the Arab World, Nov. 24, 2013. https://ballandalus.wordpress.com/2013/11/24/trans-saharan-slave-trade-and-racism-in-the-arab-world/

77   See for example MEMRI, "Islamic State (ISIS) Releases Pamphlet on Female Slaves," Dec. 4, 2014.

78   Verity Educate, p. 102-108 offers a critique of *World History: The Human Odyssey,* Jackson Spielvogel, p. 870-876, 1057-1064.

79   Holt, Rinehart, and Winston's *World History: Human Legacy* is reviewed in Education or Indoctrination? The Treatment of Islam in 6th Through 12th Grade American Textbooks, 2011, Act! For America Education, Inc.

80   *World Civilizations: The Global Experience,* Peter Stearns et al., Pearson Education, NY, 2015 p. 244-251

81   Another textbook utilized was *The Great Arab Conquests: How the Spread of Islam Changed the World We Live In,* Hugh Kennedy, DaCapo Press, Philadelphia, 2007.

82   Ira Zepp, *A Muslim Primer:Beginner's Guide to Islam,* University of Arkansas Press, 2000.

83   Zepp was a Christian scholar, but had no formal credentials as an Islamic scholar. According to his biography he graduated from Drew Theological Seminary, earned a Ph.D from St. Mary's Seminary in Baltimore, and studied theology in Edinburgh, Scotland and Gottigen, Germany, as well as at the Hebrew University in Jerusalem and the Hartford Seminary.

84   For a more scholarly discussion see an article by the Muslim Women's League, "Women in Pre-Islamic Arabia," September 1995.

A critical perspective is offered on a website called the Arab Humanist, *Arab women before and after Islam: Opening the door of pre-Islamic Arabian history*. http://www.arabhumanists.org/arab-women-pre-islam/ , "Reading all the sources now available, one can see that, in the absence of a single law before Islam, lives of men and women in Arabia depended on which tribe they belonged to. Islam did lay down comprehensive law and while some women may have enjoyed more rights under Islamic law, it is certainly true that the rights of others were severely curtailed. The resultant picture that emerges is that of a deeply patriarchal form of religious law rather than one that could have been more balanced, just and equal."

85   Zepp, p. 173.

86   The veiling of women was regarded as a sign of respectability and high status; married women wore it to distinguish themselves from women slaves and unchaste women.

87   Zepp, p. 174.

88   Ibid, p. 175.

89   Muslim Women's League, "Women in Pre-Islamic Arabia," September 1995, http://www.mwlusa.org/topics/history/herstory.html

90   Zepp, p. 172. Zepp writes, "Women's testimony is worth half of man's especially in civil cases. This is an attempt to forego distraction from family responsibilities and to protect women from the rigor and discomfort of prolonged trials. It also reflects a feeling that woman's emotional nature may prevent her from being as objective as men."

91   Ibid.

92   Yusuf Sidani, *Women, Work and Islam in Arab Societies,* American University of Beirut, March 2005. http://www.academia.edu/187671/Women_work_and_Islam_in_Arab_societies provides a detailed discussion and data on women's participation in the labor force, rates of literacy and attitudes toward women in the workplace among Islamic thinkers. Generally, women's participation in the workplace in Islamic countries lags far behind the West.

93   *Women, Business and the Law,* World Bank, 2016. http://wbl.worldbank.org/~/media/WBG/WBL/Documents/ Reports/2016/Women-Business-and-the-Law-2016.pdf

94   Other chapters allege the relatively mild treatment of religious minorities in Muslim-dominant societies, asserting that Jews and Christians appreciated coming under Muslim rule. The book also promotes the discredited story that astronaut Neil Armstrong had secretly converted to Islam.

95   *World Civilizations: The Global Experience,* "The First Global Civilization: The Rise and Spread of Islam," p. 136-137, Peter N. Stearns, Michael B. Adas, Stuart B. Schwarz and Marc Jason Gilbert, Published by Pearson 2015.

96   Mary Walker, "Where Womanhood Reigns Supreme," *Impact Magazine.*

97   "Women, Business and Law," http://wbl.worldbank.org/

The World Bank has published a series of reports on the status of women worldwide. These reports present data demonstrating a substantial gender gap in human rights, economic opportunity, and status in Muslim nations in comparison to Western nations.

98   *Religions of the World,* Breuilly, Olsen and Palmer. The selection is part of a series titled, *Illustrated Guide to Origins, Beliefs, Traditions and Festivals,* Transedition Limited and Fernleigh Books Limited, 1997-2005.

99   "Islam: An Introduction," Saudi Aramco World, January/February 2002, p. 4.

100   Unattributed photocopied handout from 9th grade World History course.

101   Bernard Lewis wrote in the *Crisis of Islam*, 2003:

The term *jihad*, conventionally translated "holy war," has the literal meaning of striving, more specifically, in the Qur'anic phrase "striving in the path of God" (*fi sabil Allah*). Some Muslim theologians, particularly in more modern times, have interpreted the duty of "striving in the path of God" in a spiritual and moral sense. The overwhelming majority of early authorities, however, citing relevant passages in the Qur'an and in the tradition, discuss jihad in military terms. Virtually every manual of shari'a law has a chapter on jihad, which regulates in minute detail such matters as the opening, conduct, interruption and cessation of hostilities, and the allocation and division of booty. Lewis concludes this passage by saying: "The object of jihad is to bring the whole world under Islamic law."

An article by Douglas Streusand in the Middle East Forum, "Islam in the textbooks," Summer 2003, p. 69, http://www.meforum.org/357/what-does-jihad-mean, includes a detailed discussion about the meaning of Jihad. Streusand writes: "Thus did three main views of jihad co-exist in premodern times: the classical legal view of jihad as a compulsory, communal effort to defend and expand Dar al-Islam; Ibn Taymiya's notion of active jihad as an indispensable feature of legitimate rule; and the Sufi doctrine of greater jihad. It is no surprise that the disagreement over jihad continues in the modern era."

102   Khaleel Mohammed, "Does Islamic scripture justify jihad violence?", *San Diego Tribune*, Dec. 15, 2015. http://www.sandiegouniontribune.com/lifestyle/people/sdut-quran-hadith-2015dec19-story.html

103   John Esposito, *Islam, the Straight Path,* p. 22.

104   Ibid, p. 22.

105   Ibid, p. 22.

106   Stephen Schwartz, *John L. Esposito: Apologist for Wahabi Islam,* American Thinker, September 18, 2011. Esposito is the founding director of the Alwaleed Center for Christian-Muslim Understanding at Georgetown University, which is funded by Saudi businessman Alwaleed bin Talal, who reportedly provided matching gifts of 20 million dollars to Georgetown University and Harvard University.

107   *Nightline,* ABC News, "The Hajj: One American's Pilgrimage to Mecca," April 18, 1997.

108   Photocopied sheet containing a passage from the textbook *World History: Connections to Today,* Prentice-Hall, 1999.

109   Photocopied sheet containing a passage from the textbook, *A Little History of the World,* E.H. Gombrich, Steyermul-Verlag, Vienna, 1936.

110   Photocopied sheet titled, Document B: Verses from the Qur'an, The DBQ Project.

111   *World Civilizations: The Global Experience,* chapter 6: The First Global Civilization: The Rise and Spread of Islam, p. 130-145, by Peter N. Stearns, Michael B. Adas, Stuart B. Schwarz and Marc Jason Gilbert, Published by Pearson 2015.

112   Photocopied handout titled "Spread of Islam Cause and Effect."

113   Desmond Stuart et. al, *Early Islam ,* Time-Life Books 1967.

114   Efraim Karsh, *Islamic Imperialism: A History,* Yale University Press, 2006, p. 26.

115   Efraim Karsh, *Islamic Imperialism,* p. 20

116   Published 2015 FBI crime statistics. U.S. https://ucr.fbi.gov/hate-crime/2015/resource-pages/download-files

117   Time Magazine, "Islamophobia: Does America Have a Muslim Problem" Aug. 30, 2010, http://content.time.com/time/magazine/article/0,9171,2011936,00.html

118   The author went on to stir further controversy with his statement that burning the Koran is worse than burning the Bible because the former is the word of God while the latter is not. http://www.mediaite.com/tv/msnbcs-hardball-guest-explains-why-burning-the-koran-is-worse-than-burning-the-bible/

119   "Student Voices: What students are saying about antisemitism on their campuses" AMCHA Initiative, Protecting Jewish Students, 2015 http://www.amchainitiative.org/student-voices-being-jewish-on-campus/

120   *Guardian,* "Disney sued for discrimination by former employee over Muslim hijab" Aug. 14, 2012.

121   *The New York Times,* "Islamic emblem of bias also trigger for bias" Nov. 3, 1997.

122   "Responding to Terrorism: Challenges for Democracy", The Choices Program, Brown University, P. 4. http://www.choices.edu/resources/detail.php?id=26

123   Ibid, p. 4.

124   *The New York Times,* "Long Hidden Details reveal cruelty of 1972 Munich Attackers," Dec. 2, 2015. The *Times* piece documented the sadism of the hijackers, discrediting the claims by the leader of the group that they did not intend to kill the hostages. The hijackers castrated one of the hostages.

125   Responding to Terrorism, p. 11.

126   Responding to Terrorism, p. 15.

127   Verity Educate, p. 19.

128   Ibid, p. 19-34.

129   Crisis Guide: Israeli-Palestinian Conflict (Interactive), Council on Foreign Relations, Chapter II: The Territorial Puzzle, http://www.cfr.org/israel/crisis-guide-israeli-palestinian-conflict/p13850

130   *Religions of the World*, Edited by Breuilly, O'Brien, Palmer, produced for Fernleigh books Limited and Transedition Limited by Bender, Richardson and White, 2005 edition. This book discusses tensions between modern Islam and the Western world.

131   MEMRI offers insights into the Middle East and South Asia through their media by bridging the language gap with the West. It provides translations of Arabic, Faris, Urdu-Pashtu, Dari and Turkish media as well as analysis of political, ideological, intellectual, social, cultural and religious trends. http://www.memri.org/about-memri.html.

132   PMW is an Israeli research institute that studies Palestinian society by monitoring and analyzing the Palestinian Authority through its media and schoolbooks. PMW's major focus is on the messages that Palestinian leaders, from the Palestinian Authority, Fatah and Hamas, send to the population through the broad range of institutions and infrastructures they control. https://www.palwatch.org/

Part 4: Origins of Factually Flawed Materials

The problem of inaccurate and biased material in the teaching of Islam, the Middle East, and the Israeli-Palestinian conflict in American schools has been recognized at least as far back as the 1970s.[1] Initially, the focus was on the accuracy and completeness of textbook accounts. Later, increased attention was paid to supplemental materials derived from a variety of sources, including outreach centers and Internet sites. The use of these materials has been widespread for decades.

A. Biased Textbooks

Although there is increasing utilization of Internet sources and supplemental materials, textbooks still provide the factual foundation for many students in World History courses teaching about Islam. Textbook chapters usually are organized to cover the emergence, elements of practice, and spread of Islam. These chapters include basic historical facts and important dates.

Bernard Lewis

By the late 1980s, educators were aware of serious problems of accuracy and bias in textbooks that dealt with Islam and the Middle East conflicts. The first edition of the *Arab World Studies Notebook* was published in 1989.

Gilbert Sewall, director of the American Textbook Council, reviewed the coverage of Islam in American school textbooks in 2003. Sewall concluded "on significant Islam-related subjects, textbooks omit, flatter, embellish, and resort to happy talk, suspending criticism or harsh judgments that would raise provocative or even alarming questions."[2]

Sewall drew upon the expertise of Bernard Lewis to evaluate textbooks on their coverage of fundamental aspects of Islamic history and society. These include accurate depictions of jihad, Sharia law, slavery under Islam and the status of women.

Sewall recounted how both Harvard University's Outreach Center and a Brown University professor involved with Middle East outreach criticized Massachusetts standards as "racist and biased" simply because the standards included accurate discussion of elements of Islamic practice and history and did not filter out unpleasant aspects.

Sewall's study points out that the problem with most textbooks comes down to two main issues. First, there is a tendency to portray non-Western historical narratives with rose-colored glasses. "Multiculturalism and 'cross-cultural sensitivity' trump all other themes in today's social studies and civic education." Thus, doctored curricula and altered world history textbooks prevail.[3]

Second, publishers seek to mollify pressure groups. Sewall pointed to the influence of the Council on Islamic Education, a group with foreign associations and Islamist roots. He noted that "high-profile publishers and editors at Houghton Mifflin, Scott Foresman, Glencoe, and Prentice Hall asked for the Council on Islamic Education imprimatur between 1987 and 1997."[4] The impact on the content and direction of history textbooks during these years is still evident even today.

While Sewall's study is over a decade old, problems with content in history textbooks remain. William Saxton of Concerned Citizens for National Security heads an organization that is particularly active in addressing problems with textbooks. Saxton estimates that he fields about six inquiries related to inaccuracies in textbooks on the subject of Islam and the Arab-Israeli conflict every day. These include "sins of omission and commission." Examples of this are statements like "war broke out between Palestinians and Israelis" without clarifying who initiated the violence; concealing realities of Islamic history, like Islam's role in the slave trade; and describing Jesus as a "Palestinian."[5]

The national Jewish organization Hadassah sponsored a project called Curriculum Watch,[6] which was tasked with evaluating textbooks published by the major educational publishing houses for bias against Jews and other minorities and also with identifying sections that "sanitize" one group of people or events. The director of Curriculum Watch, Sandra Alfonsi, set up an independent website that contains her evaluations of textbooks for anti-Israel bias.[7]

There is increasing recognition nationwide of the problem of slanted textbooks that whitewash Islamic traditions and offer negative portrayals of Judaism and Christianity. Alfonsi is slated to serve on a newly proposed New York State Textbook Commission.[8] The commission is to review textbooks in an effort to make the school curriculum in New York State fair to all students and free of any bias toward Islamic traditions and against Judaeo/Christian values.

The historical accounts presented in the textbooks are influenced by the academics that textbook publishers draw upon for their expertise. The academics are in turn influenced by the ideological and intellectual trends prevalent at universities. Especially influential are Centers for Middle East and Islamic studies. These Centers often are the beneficiaries of substantial funding from groups promoting partisan political agendas as well as the federal government. As cultural commentator Stanley Kurtz observed in 2007, "The United States government gives money — and a federal seal of approval — to a university Middle East Studies center. That center offers a government-approved K-12 Middle East studies curriculum to America's teachers. But, in fact, that curriculum has been bought and paid for by the Saudis, who may even have trained the personnel who operate the university's outreach program."[9]

B. Funding of Academic Departments Favoring Islamic Perspectives

Generous funding of Centers for Middle Eastern and Islamic studies comes from two major sources:

1) Arab states, grown wealthy from their oil resources[10], and

2) The U.S. government.[11]

The vehicle used to bolster the teaching of Islam, the Middle East, and the Arab-Israeli conflict in K-12 history curricula was Title VI funding of the Higher Education Act (HEA), an Act originally passed in 1958 by the United States Congress. Public outreach was required by Congress as part of each grant to a higher education institution.

After the terrorist attacks of September 11, 2001, considerably more funding was made available through Title VI to teach about Islam and the Middle East. In a speech at the Islamic Center in Washington just six days after the attacks, President George W. Bush affirmed that "the face of terror is not the true faith of Islam. Islam is peace."[12]

Taking its cue from the President's words, the U.S. Department of Education (USED) ramped up federal funding of Middle East studies and language programs. The goal was to increase Americans' understanding of Islam. It was hoped that this would enhance interactions with Muslim communities at home and abroad and help prevent future attacks by depriving Islamic radicals of a receptive audience to their exhortations to violence.

Unfortunately, oversight of the program has been lax. The recipients of these funds interpreted the President's message according to their own predilections. An anti-Western zeitgeist pervaded Middle East Studies departments at universities. Faculty members recognized an opportunity to address what they saw as the main problems: Western intrusion into the Middle East and prejudice against Muslims in America. Understanding and addressing the links between terrorism and Islam was not high on their agenda.

A study published by Brandeis University in 2014, "The Morass of Middle East Studies: Title VI of the Higher Education Act and Federally Funded Area Studies," concluded that Title VI programs to improve secondary school teaching of the Middle East "had become a national embarrassment."[13] The study noted:

> Title VI programs became controversial for many perceived shortcomings. These included: the relatively weak knowledge, skills, and standards of many Middle East Studies faculty; the ideological polarization of the field; and the failure of Middle East Studies scholars to predict important area developments, such as the Iranian revolution, the September 11, 2001 attacks, or the Arab Spring.

Disappointment with the results of Title VI funding of Middle East Studies programs is widely acknowledged. This may have influenced the Obama administration's decision to cut funding to the program by 40% in 2011.[14]

The Brandeis study disclosed deep problems with Middle East Studies departments. Gary A. Tobin, at the Institute for Jewish and Community Research, observed:

> The field of Middle East Studies has become dominated by a specific political outlook that situates the world and everyone in it according to a narrow agenda. Poor scholarship, due to errors of both commission and omission, plagues the work of Middle East Studies faculty, including revisionism in rewriting the history of Israel and Jews. As a result, some students and faculty have found that they are marginalized because of their religion, nationality, or political beliefs. Students can be made to feel as if their views are invalid, or even bigoted. Some have reported being directly harassed by professors. [15]

Tobin argued that Middle East Studies programs are "at the forefront of the anti-Israel movement" and even "engage in anti-Semitic behavior."[16] A recent example of this is a course taught at the University of California in Berkeley by Hatem Bazian, a vociferous proponent of anti-Israel boycotts who advocates the dissolution of the Jewish state.[17] A complaint brought by the AMCHA Initiative and a coalition representing 43 groups contended that "all class reading material appears to have a 'blatantly anti-Israel bias' and use language recognized by the U.S. State Department as anti-Semitic."[18] In its initial review, the university concluded that the course violated the University Regents' policies. However, shortly afterwards, the university reversed its decision and reinstated the course to counter the criticism it violated the principle of academic freedom.[19]

Another example of academic anti-Israel activism is the classroom conduct of professor Denis Sullivan at Northeastern University, who at one time was on the faculty of the Jewish Studies department.[20] Students taking his class report on his anti-Israel agenda. Those who dare to contest his views report that they have been demeaned, humiliated, and even threatened with poor grades unless they change their position. Sullivan has assigned readings conveying to students the belief that a Jewish lobby controls American foreign policy, and he can be seen on video asserting that Hamas is a legitimate resistance organization.[21]

Sullivan chaired Paul Beran's dissertation. Beran then went on to head Harvard's Outreach Center and was selected to participate in the Global Advisory Council for the Massachusetts Department of Education, which advised state education officials on teaching about global issues, like Islam and the Israeli-Palestinian conflict.[22] The Harvard University Center for Middle Eastern Studies received a half million dollars per year in Title VI funding. [23] Northeastern University's Sullivan is also a recipient of Title VI funding.[24]

The transformation of academic departments into enclaves of political orthodoxy is a familiar story in many social science and humanities disciplines. Faculty committed to promoting an anti-Western and anti-Israel agenda were ascendant in most departments by the 1990s, if not earlier. Having gained control of faculty appointments and tenure decisions, they imposed conformity of thought. Those unwilling to embrace the prevailing ideology were deterred from pursuing academic appointments. In this way, the orthodoxy became self-perpetuating. [25]

The narrow ideological base of Middle East studies has not escaped notice. A 2016 review of Title VI funding by the National Academies Press noted the objections of a few prominent researchers that a "lack of diversity of opinion and a hostility to U.S. foreign policy" existed in Middle East studies.[26] Evidence of this can be found in the radical composition and politics of MESA, the Middle East Studies Association.[27]

Joy Pullmann, managing editor of the *Federalist*, an online blog site that covers current events and culture, has written about the insidious effects of the infusion of foreign money into the universities. According to Pullmann, employees of institutes receiving such money avoid topics critical of Islamic society for fear of their reputations and employment.[28]

Winfield Myers, director of academic affairs at the Middle East Forum, told Pullmann that Saudi money in American higher education "gives incentives for not asking critical questions." This avoidance of anything critical of Islamic society "motivates curriculum companies to similarly downplay religious and racial conflict, at the expense of accuracy and substance." [29]

Anti-Israel activism by a Muslim student on the campus of Brooklyn College commemorating a terrorist who attempted to hijack an El Al plane

Pullmann points to the example of Susan Douglass, who runs an outreach program for a center affiliated with Georgetown University, the beneficiary of one of the $20 million gifts by Saudi prince Alwaleed Bin Talal. According to Pullmann, Douglass traverses the country giving seminars at school districts and conferences where she promotes materials claiming that "customs such as honor killings are not part of Islam" and that "Jihad may not be conducted either to force people to convert or to annihilate or subdue people of other faiths."[30]

C. Internet

The emergence of the Internet as a source of curriculum materials presents its own problems. As the Newton case study demonstrates, many of the objectionable materials were found on the Internet, presumably by individual teachers. Some of these materials originate from well-known media organizations, like the BBC, *The New York Times*, and PBS. Others were taken from less familiar Internet sources.

Journalists are not generally trained as historians and should not be viewed as authoritative purveyors of history. Many present a skewed perspective on the Israeli-Palestinian conflict, including at AP, as CAMERA has repeatedly demonstrated over the past 34 years.[31] Problems with factual accuracy afflict even the best-known news outlets like *The New York Times*,[32] BBC,[33] and National Public Radio.[34]

Wire services, which many newspapers rely on, have also been criticized for their biased coverage of the Palestinian/Israeli conflict. For example, former Associated Press (AP) correspondent Matti Friedman has described journalists covering the Israeli-Palestinian conflict as a clique possessing a deeply ingrained bias: [35]

> In these circles...a distaste for Israel has come to be something between an acceptable prejudice and a prerequisite for entry. I don't mean a critical approach to Israeli policies or to the ham-fisted government currently in charge in this country, but a belief that to some extent the Jews of Israel are a symbol of the world's ills, particularly those connected to nationalism, militarism, colonialism, and racism—an idea quickly becoming one of the central elements of the "progressive" Western *zeitgeist*, spreading from the European left to American college campuses and intellectuals, including journalists. In this social group, this sentiment is translated into editorial decisions made by individual reporters and editors covering Israel, and this, in turn, gives such thinking the means of mass self-replication.

By relying on journalists who may have limited knowledge of Middle East history, the Israeli-Palestinian conflict, and Islam, teachers may inadvertently disseminate erroneous information or magnify the importance of contemporary issues that a journalist has been assigned to cover. This was the case in the use of the *New York Times* video series utilized by the 10th grade World History course at Newton South high school. The journalists who produced the work narrowly focused on issues that loomed large in the current discourse of their own narrow circles, but they failed to provide the factual content and broader historical perspective necessary for students to understand how the subject covered in the video was connected to the conflict as a whole. Nor did they provide a balanced perspective.

Similarly, the timeline used in the 10th grade course was produced by an intern at the Council of Foreign Relations and obtained by Newton teachers from a PBS website. It presented an incomplete recounting of key historical events.

The *Time Magazine* article and the *Guardian* piece promoting the notion of rampant Islamophobia were journalistic opinion pieces offering minimal context or factual substance to allow students to evaluate the pervasiveness of bigotry against Muslims. They offered little or no educational value to students.

1   Gary A. Tobin and Dennis R. Ybarra, *The Trouble with Textbooks: Distorting History and Religion*, Lexington Books, 2008.

2   Gilbert Sewall, *Islam and the Textbooks, A Report of the American Textbook Council*, 2003, p. 23. http://files.eric. ed.gov/fulltext/ED475822.pdf

3   Ibid. p. 31.

4   Ibid, p. 27.

5   See Joy Pullmann, TheFederalist.com, "What Do American Schools Teach About islam? PC or Nothing," August 16, 2016.

6   Curriculum Watch, http://www.hadassah.org/advocate/curriculum-watch.html?referrer=https://www.google.com/

7   http://textbookalert.com

8   *Long Island Local News,* February 26, 2016. http://lilocalnews.com/2016/02/26/curran-announces-formation-of-textbook-commission/

9   Stanley Kurtz, "Saudi auspices. Game, set, match: Saudis." July 25, 2007. http://www.nationalreview.com/article/221607 Islam in the Classroom.

10   For example, Harvard University and Georgetown University both received reported $20 million gifts from Saudi Prince Talal Bin Al Waleed in 2005 for their Centers for Middle East Studies. The University of Arkansas established the King Fahd Center after receiving a substantial donation from the government of Saudi Arabia. The University of Texas and University of California at Berkeley have also received substantial funds from Gulf Arab states. The Islamic Republic of Iran has also donated to a number of American and British programs. https://secularzionist.wordpress.com/college-campuses/funding-middle-east-programs/ A similar funding situation for Middle East studies exists at British universities.

11   A compendium of articles on the topic of bias in Middle East Studies programs and Title VI funding is available at Campus Watch, http://www.campus-watch.org/survey.php/id/48

12   "Islam is Peace", https://georgewbush-whitehouse.archives.gov/news/releases/2001/09/20010917-11.html

13   *The Morass of Middle East Studies: Title VI of the Higher Education Act and Federally Funded Area Studies,* Brandeis University, November, 2014, p. 3, http://brandeiscenter.com/images/uploads/practices/antisemitism_whitepaper.pdf

14   Martin Kramer, "A smokescreen for Palestine-pushers," Nov. 4, 2014. http://martinkramer.org/sandbox/tag/title-vi/

15   *The Morass of Middle East Studies,* p. 9. Gary A. Tobin, Aryeh K. Weinberg, Jenna Ferer. *The Uncivil University* (San Francisco: Institute for Jewish & Community Research, 2005) provides a more detailed discussion of this problem.

16   *The Morass of Middle East Studies,* p. 10.

17   Richard Cravatts, "Perverting college coursework to conform to Ideology", http://spme.org/campus-news-climate/perverting-college-coursework-conform-ideology/23291/

18   *The College Fix,* "UC-Berkeley halts class that critics say advocates the elimination of Israel" Sept. 14. 2016 http://www.thecollegefix.com/post/29007/

19   Inside Higher Ed, Sept. 20, 2016. https://www.insidehighered.com/news/2016/09/20/palestine-course-berkeley-reinstated-after-criticisms-violating-academic-freedom

20   Review of Sullivan's courses by Canary Mission, a group that exposes anti-Semitism at U.S. universities. https://canarymission.org/professors/denis-sullivan/https://canarymission.org/professors/denis-sullivan/

21   Spero News, "Investigation into Anti-Semitism ensues at Northeastern University", Aug. 21,2013. http://www.speroforum.com/a/MPFWAH0XCU46/74251-Investigation-into-antiSemitism-ensues-at-Northeastern-University-.WAegYuArIdU

22   http://www.doe.mass.edu/boe/docs/fy2011/2010-10/candidates.pdf

23   CMES newsletter, Fall 2010.

24   Denis Sullivan's resume indicates extensive grant support from Title VI among others. http://www.bu.edu/pardeeschool/files/2016/02/Denis-Sullivan-CV-Dec-2015.pdf

25   Daniel Pipes, "Middle Eastern Studies: What went wrong?" Middle East Forum, Winter 1995-96. http://www.danielpipes.org/392/middle-eastern-studies-what-went-wrong

26   *International Education and Foreign Languages: Keys to Securing Our Future* p.22, The National Academies Press, 2016. https://www.nap.edu/read/11841/chapter/4 - 22https://www.nap.edu/read/11841/chapter

27   Algemeiner, Nov. 22, 2016, "Expert: Blatant Anti-Israel Slant 'Suicidal' for Reputation, Continuity of Mideast Scholars Association." https://www.algemeiner.com/2016/11/22/expert-blatant-anti-israel-slant-suicidal-for-reputation-continuity-of-mideast-scholars-association/

28   Joy Pullmann, "What do American schools teach about Islam? PC or Nothing." http://thefederalist.com/2016/08/16/what-do-american-schools-teach-about-islam-pc-or-nothing/

29   Ibid.

30   Ibid.

31   CAMERA's website can be found at www.camera.org

32 *Indicting Israel, New York Times Coverage of the Palestinian-Israeli Conflict,* 2012, CAMERA monograph. http://www.camera.org/images_user/pdf/final monograph.pdf

33 BBC Watch, website that monitors BBC coverage of Israel. https://bbcwatch.org/

34 CAMERA coverage of NPR, http://www.camera.org/index.asp?x_context=4&x_outlet=28

35 *The Atlantic,* "What the Media Gets Wrong About Israel," Nov. 30, 2014. http://www.theatlantic.com/international/archive/2014/11/how-the-media-makes-the-israel-story/383262/

Part 5: Observations About The Newton Curriculum Conflict

A. The Role of Responsible Elected Bodies

The Newton school controversy escalated after members of the elected school committee sided with the school administrators, leaving a group of concerned citizens without representation.[1] Videos of the Newton School Committee meetings show that the superintendent was evasive in his answers. By siding with the superintendent, the school committee relieved their most senior employee of the responsibility of providing a substantive response to valid complaints about the materials.

Because the school committee aligned itself with the school administration, the ad-hoc group felt compelled to involve the mayor, who had expressed interest in school problems.[2]

The school administrators and school committee were also unresponsive to requests for access to teaching materials used in classrooms. State statutes allow any citizen, not just parents, access to all materials teachers use with students.[3] In those cases where school administrations and school committees refuse to cooperate, as was the case in Newton, filing a Freedom of Information Act request may be the only remedy.[4]

There are usually established procedures for lodging complaints and providing supporting evidence about the curriculum. The Newton Public Schools' published statement on the controversy includes a section labeled "What happens if parents or citizens have concerns about the curriculum?" It states that "Questions or concerns about specific elements of the curriculum should be brought to appropriate administrators at the building level."[5]

However, if the complainants are unsatisfied with the response of the school administrators, they should be able to bring their complaints to the school committee. An elected school committee (or board) is responsible to both its constituents and to those it has hired. It should have procedures for involving individuals with expertise in the topic to review controversial materials.[6] It is the responsibility of a locally elected school board to invite a range of well-regarded experts to help a board understand a controversy about curriculum materials.

Calling upon experts from the outside who are unaffected by the opinions of influential members of the community can provide a dispassionate assessment.

B. The Role of the Media

All meetings on curriculum issues should be open to the public. All forms of media should be invited to attend school committee meetings. An interested and involved media can bring transparency to curriculum decisions, and, in so doing, reduce the influence of special interests that prefer less scrutiny. The media can also offset the inclination of influential members of the community to squelch discussions that threaten to embroil the community in conflict and garner unwanted publicity.[7]

In Newton, there was minimal involvement of the media. The local newspaper played an important role in publicizing the initial complaint. However, as the controversy evolved, the local newspaper curtailed its coverage, rejecting requests to publish opinion pieces on the issue. It is unclear why the newspaper decided to back away from an issue important to the local community.

With respect to the Newton controversy, the major regional paper, the *Boston Globe* delved into the issue only a couple of occasions, coming down firmly on the side of the established institutions. The *Globe's* refusal to probe the issue further was a disservice to the public.

Some local radio talk shows discussed the issue on several occasions, accepting phone calls and inviting some of the activists and concerned citizens to comment on the situation.

As far as is known, television news never covered the issue at all.

C. The Focus on Current Events in Teaching History

Many of the problems with teaching materials would not have existed (because the materials would not have been used) if the Newton history courses had focused only on the history of Islam and the Middle East and had not given special attention to the conflict between Israelis and Palestinians. Many of the materials used to address the Israeli-Palestinian conflict were marred by biased historical accounts. As a result, students spent time on materials that could not help them understand the roots of radical Islamic ideology. Exercises that ask pre-college students to role-play the lives and beliefs of other people in the world are of dubious value in any context and cannot replace factual content.

The use of the World History course to acquaint students with a contemporary politically-contentious issue complicates the task of teaching world history. Much of the materials selected by teachers is sound. However, the wide array of sources available on the internet and from academic workshops invites the intrusion of political partisanship into the teaching of history.

Unfortunately, U.S. public schools are increasingly allowing the teaching of Islamic and Middle East history to be influenced by non-scholarly media commentaries and partisan individuals and groups. Although the concerned citizens in Newton still do not feel their School Committee wants to listen to them, there has been some change in the selection of materials. It seems likely that the publicity stimulated by the controversy has prompted more thoughtful selection of materials and more careful vetting of them than occurred previously. The materials provided in the FOIA requests did not include some of the most biased and academically unsuitable items examined in 2011 through 2014.[8] Moreover, publishers are beginning to respond to concerns about their texts.[9] Still, the supplemental materials continue to favor fringe perspectives[10] at the expense of mainstream historians and include mainly unscholarly sources presenting distorted and incomplete information.

Some of the initial problems in the selection of materials were a consequence of the early involvement of some Newton educators with the Outreach Center at Harvard University and their attendance at other Middle East workshops promoting or giving away biased materials. Examination of the materials used in the different classes revealed that individual teachers relied on different sources. As a result, some classes included more of the problematic materials discussed in this monograph, and others less. Furthermore, the unit on the Palestinian/Israeli conflict was only taught in some classes and not in others.

The ad-hoc citizens' group, APT, and PENS helped to expose the biased Outreach Center and kept Newton educators and the school committee from relying further on such compromised sources. School committees and boards everywhere need to develop acceptable procedures for selecting teaching materials and for addressing community concerns about the materials used in K-12 curricula.

The importance of continued involvement by parents and community groups cannot be overstated. Organizations seeking to advance their social and political agendas increasingly promote their educational materials to school systems under the rubric of pursuing peace and cultural engagement, and countering bigotry. However, woven into the curricular materials are dubious facts and spurious allegations. For example, one education curriculum available online contends that "Islamophobia" in the United States is the result of "scare tactics" disseminated by a "well-financed and organized Islamophobic movement." [11]

To underscore the challenge that lies ahead, it is worth noting that the Family Foundation of Betsy Devos, Secretary of Education in the U.S. Department of Education, is a major funder of educational initiatives promoting a social studies curriculum on the Arab world and the Middle East whose stated goal is to

> "remind educators and students alike to look beneath the surface, to question preconceived notions and prejudices on the journey to global citizenship."[12]

While such humanitarian aspirations seem laudable, the fear is that an accurate fact-based teaching of history may be sacrificed so that students can question "preconceived prejudices." Reference to "global citizenship" too may suggest a continuing shift away from focus on the unique and important contributions of the West and America.

Finally, students must be allowed to address contemporary problems with Islamic society in a critical manner if the development of "critical thinking skills" is a genuine goal of the curriculum. This means allowing students to learn, for example, that indoctrination to hate Jews – as well as other non-Muslim minorities elsewhere in the Middle East – may be a crucial reason for the perpetuation of the Israeli-Palestinian conflict. Exposing such a reality should be seen as beneficial – not harmful – for students as it illuminates a significant dimension of the world that awaits all of them, a world that will need their sound, informed judgement and insight to navigate.

1   This perspective was provided by several members of the ad-hoc group in 2016 in independent interviews.

2   PENS website.

3   Massachusetts Public Records Law (MPRL), G.L. c.4, 7(26) and G.L.c.66, 10.

4   Judicial Watch submitted a FOIA request on October 2014. Newton began providing materials in May 2015.

5   Newton Public Schools: History Curriculum Statement.

6   This might also avoid unnecessary consequences like involving students in the controversy. On April 21, 2014, a local newspaper printed a letter signed by 478 Newton students defending the teachers from the charges of being "anti-Israel" or of "glorifying Islam." The tone and content of the letter raised suspicion among some that the letter was not strictly the initiative of the students. Some suspected the students had been manipulated by ideologically-motivated teachers.

7   *Boston Globe*, "Rabbi says bias forum took a bad turn," April 20, 2016. More than four years after the controversy broke, the rabbi of Newton's largest synagogue told a *Boston Globe* reporter that "he doesn't consider the curriculum question to be a real issue," although he admitted he had not looked closely into the matter.

8   For example, the pages copied from the Internet site, Islamicweb.com, that were sharply criticized by the Verity Educate report do not appear in the 2015 materials. The chapter by UCLA professor James Gelvin and the *Flashpoints* handouts also were not included in the 2015 materials.

9   In early 2016, McGraw Hill recalled a textbook containing the series of four chronological maps disseminated by the PLO Information Office described in this monograph.

10   At the universities, academics are fighting back against the anti-Israel and anti-Western bias in Middle East studies departments. What makes this battle particularly challenging is that some of the most recognizable names in academia are among the most notorious purveyors of biased accounts and unsubstantiated facts. An example of this was recently exposed in an article discussing a false claim by Columbia University's Rashid Khalidi, who once served as a spokesperson for the PLO. Another example is the oft-quoted anti-Zionist Ilan Pappe.

11   Islamic Networks Group (ING), section of website devoted to discussing "Islamophobia."

12   Bridges to Understanding is underwritten by the Betsy and Dick Devos Family Foundation. Its mission statement states: To foster a personal understanding between the American people and the people of the Arab World. https://bridgesofunderstanding.org/about-us/

Attachments

Attachment 1: A handout used in a Newton class in 2011 that contained erroneous information

FLASHPOINTS: Guide to World Conflicts

Country Briefing

Israel-Palestine

Overview

After more than 50 years of war, terrorism, peace negotiation and human suffering, Israel and Palestine remain as far from a peaceful settlement as ever. The entire Middle Eastern region remains a cauldron waiting to reach the boiling point, a potent mixture of religious extremism, (Jewish, Christian and Islamic), mixed with oil and munitions.

The Israeli-Palestinian conflict is a major source of Arab and Muslim grievances against the West in general and the US in particular. Over recent decades, Israel has continuously strengthened its influence over American domestic politics and Middle East policy.

Up until 2000, the US was often seen as an independent broker, working to resolve the Mid-East conflict, but in recent years America has abdicated any role in negotiating a peace agreement, while lending tacit support to unilateral Israeli policies in the Occupied Territories. Failure to resolve the Israeli-Palestinian conflict continues to fuel Islamic extremism throughout the Middle East and is a root cause behind Al-Qaeda's war against Israel and the West.

Middle East Instability

For most people, the Mid-East Crisis has been a fixture on the world political stage for the entire lifetime, from the Arab-Israeli wars to plane hijackings, the Munich Olympic massacre and a seemingly endless series of shuttle diplomacy. Over five decades Israel has grown size, wealth and power, defeating Arab armies and has become a nuclear power able to dominate the region. Meanwhile, Palestinians remain in refugee camps, resigned to poverty, a people without a country and without hope. The Palestinians have fought back with stones, terrorism and suicide bombs, only to face collective punishment at the hands of the Israeli Defense Forces (IDF).

Capital: Tel Aviv
Area: 21,060 sq km
Pop: 6,967,000

Capital: Jerusalem
Area: 6,220 sq km
Pop:3,945,000

During this time we have witnessed the rise and fall of communism, pan-Arabism and Saddam Hussein's Iraq. We've seen the Islamic Revolution in Iran, the advent of globalization and the Internet, but Israel and Palestine remain gridlocked. Today, frustration and anger spawned by years of hypocrisy, exploitation and political failure have unleashed a new variant of international terrorism on America and Europe. Although Palestine is a root cause of today's international terrorism, little, if anything, is being done to find a path to peaceful settlement.

History

Home Page

Conflict Briefings

Issue Briefings

Insight & Analysis

Dispatches

Marketplace

The ancient city of Jerusalem is a religious center of Judaism, Islam and Christianity and the surrounding region of Palestine reflects this religious diversity. In the late 1800's, a Zionist movement began seeking the creation of a Jewish homeland and state in Palestine, at that time part of the Turkish Ottoman Empire. At the end of World War I, the Ottoman Empire was divided into independent states and colonial jurisdictions. Palestine was placed under control of Britain, which issued the Balfour Declaration, promising a Jewish homeland and vowing protection of rights for non-Jewish peoples in Palestine.

While Syria, Lebanon, Iraq and Jordan gained independence; Britain retained control of Palestine. The Zionist movement encouraged the migration of Jews to Israel, altering the demographics of Palestine, which had been about 90% Arab. As Britain attempted to control the Jewish migration, Jewish activists supported illegal immigration and the "Irgun" emerged as a guerrilla force, opposed to British rule. Jewish settlers purchased land from wealthy Arab landowners, expelled Arab peasants and established communal colonies (Kibbutzim), protected by armed militias.

The Holocaust of World War II united the Jewish Diaspora and focused international attention on the plight of persecuted Jews. In 1947, reacting to increasing anti-British terrorist attacks by Irgun, Britain sought intervention by the United Nations, and devised a partition plan, establishing independent Arab and Jewish territories, under UN administration. Led by Menachem Begin, the Irgun quickly launched a campaign to consolidate areas under Jewish control, while Arab states threatened invasion. In 1948, the British withdrew and Ben Gurion proclaimed the independent state of Israel, provoking an invasion by Arab armies. The war lasted until 1949 and left Israel in control of 40% more

70

Attachment 2: *A Muslim Primer: Beginner's Guide to Islam*

The Status of Women

Paradise lies at the feet of mothers. (Hadith)

All human beings (male and female) are equal, equal as the teeth of a comb. There is no superiority of a white over a black nor of any male over the female. Only the God-consciousness (regardless of gender) merit favor and the ultimate rewards from God. (Muhammad)

With the possible exception of Jihad, the place of women in Islam is the most misunderstood notion by westerners. To be sure, Saudi Arabia, a few Gulf States, and increasingly Sudan and Pakistan combine their strong patriarchal tradition with the most conservative interpretation of Islamic law regarding women. As a result, from a western point of view, women often face unusual discrimination. But it should be said at the outset that the treatment of women in these countries is less a reflection of the Quran and more an expression of a cultural tradition which has inevitably been deferential to men.

Women's place in Muslim countries is as complex an issue as the status of women in Christian countries. A discussion of women and Islam must be seen in the context of class, country, and above all, the Quran. It is more accurate to say what a particular country does not permit women to do than to say what Islam permits or forbids.

The latter half of the twentieth century has seen a revival of extremely reactionary movements in Muslim countries, especially in and around the Middle East. Whenever that happens, women have often lost the status to which the Quran elevated them. Conversations with persons who have spent part of the last decade in Pakistan, Sudan, Egypt, and Arab Gulf States have confirmed this. Saudi Arabia and Iran represent this trend also.

But we hear little about the diversity of women's opportunities in Islamic countries and the flexibility of Islam as it moves from patriarchal cultures to democratic countries to the matriarchal societies of Indonesia and sub-Saharan Africa. We hear less about how women's traditional place is changing, what the Quran really says about women, and how many Muslim women are doctors, computer scientists, engineers, teachers, and bankers. The prominence of "class" in determining the destiny of Muslim women is also ignored. The poverty of most Muslim families compound whatever other religious and political status women might have.

The Quran and Women: Historical Context

Two-thirds of women in pre–Islamic society were slaves. They had no rights or legal and social status. Female infanticide was common. Men could have an unlimited number of wives and divorce them for no apparent reason with impunity. Inheritance always went to adult male relatives.

Islam and the Quran created major improvements in the status of women. They were oases in a desert of misogyny. The Quranic ideals, however, were not always translated into practice. The relative emancipation of women found in Islamic scripture has been seriously diluted by longstanding habits of male domination and cultural attitudes. Judaism and Christianity do not need reminding that cultural and secular interests can prevail over religious values.

Non–Muslim and Muslim societies forget the strong women of the early Islamic period—the successful business woman Khadija, the religious influence of Aisha and Fatima—and the fact that women participated in the army in early Islam. Allah was so concerned about the place of women that there is more said in the Quran about that than any other social issue. One of the longest Suras is entitled "Women" and in this case, the title represents the main content of the chapter.

The Quran and Women: Echo of Culture

There was in the Quran, just as in every divine text of major world religions, a reflection of cultural devaluation of women which appears restrictive and discriminatory to many Muslim and Western women.

1. Women's testimony is worth half of man's especially in civil cases. This is an attempt to forego distraction from family responsibilities and to protect women from the rigor and discomfort of prolonged trials. It also reflects a feeling that woman's emotional nature may prevent her from being as objective as men. On the other hand, in criminal cases, a woman's testimony carries as much weight as a man's.

2. Her share of inheritance is one-half of a male relative in the same category. This apparent inequity is justified because men have the obligation to provide for a family and will need extra income. Since women may keep whatever dowry they receive, there is a hope that income level will ultimately be fair. (See 4:7-12, 176)

3. There is no polyandry (more than one husband), but polygyny (more than one wife) has continued.

4. The husband is the head of the household, is the final authority, and has due obedience and cooperation from his wife. If the wife is rebellious or disobedient, there are several options open to the husband. He may first try to dissuade her with kind and gentle reasoning. If this fails, he

may then refrain from sleeping with her. And if the above are not effective, he has the Quranic permission to "beat her slightly." (4:34)

Such "slight physical correction" (Yusuf Ali) avoids her face and other sensitive areas. Striking your wife in the face (as was pictured in the film *Not Without My Daughter*) and other forms of verbal and physical cruelty have no sanction in the Quran. Many Muslims feel that although permitted, this activity is not advisable and is the exception much more than the rule.

If all else fails, the next verse (35) suggests the couple seek help and counsel from a mediator. Perhaps the disagreement between husband and wife can be resolved in this open, balanced, and neutral way.[21]

Seclusion   and   the   Veil

In the traditional societies of the Middle East, women are not socially independent. They need men to act on their behalf. They ask men's permission to leave home; and they are often secluded from male visitors to the home. Women cannot be imams, although they can lead prayer services for women in their homes. On the other hand, Sufi societies allow women to be religious leaders and are generally more positive about all aspects of womanhood.

The aforementioned reference to seclusion needs some elaboration. It is often called "veiling" or *purdah*, another word for seclusion. The rigidity with which it is held depends on the country involved. It is most prevalent in Saudi Arabia, Afghanistan, and post-revolutionary Iran, but to some degree it is present in most Muslim societies. Actually, purdah and complete veiling are Persian and Indian customs which, in time, many neighboring countries adopted. There is one verse in the Quran which mentions veiling: "Prophet, enjoin your wives, your daughters, and the wives of true believers to draw their veils close round them. That is more proper so they may be recognized and not molested." (35:59 also 24:30-31) The historical context for what is "proper" is that Arabian women before Islam were scantily attired and often topless; as a result, they were abused by men.

The primary concern of the Quran is modesty in dress. "Drawing the veil close round them" had the intention of preventing promiscuity and arousing men's desire, but most of all it guarded against disrespect of women and violence against them.

Although "veiling" is barely mentioned in the Quran, it is a form of status among contemporary wealthy educated Egyptian women to wear a *ghata*, a kind of scarf which exposes only the face. For others in Iran and Saudi Arabia, where most of the body is covered, it is a matter of religious obedience.

Jane Smith, formerly of Harvard Center for the Study of World Religions and now Dean of Academic Affairs at Iliff School of Theology of Denver, has a helpful perspective on why Muslim women dress the way they do:

Regardless of their degree of liberation, Muslim women value modesty as well as prize and retain their femininity. They find particularly odious, as do Muslim men, the sexual permissiveness of Western society. Whether the control exercised by Muslim men over their women is viewed as protection or exploitation, the fact remains that liberal and conservative Muslims alike are appalled and disgusted by women's open display of themselves and the sexual freedoms seen as part of the general emancipation of women in the West.... To cite the expressive commentary of Fatima Mernissi, "While Muslim exploitation of the female is clad under veils and buried behind walls, Western exploitation has the bad taste of being unclad, bare and overexposed."*2

* It would be only fair to record that Muslims see Christianity as counseling women also to be obedient, modest in dress, submissive to husbands, and quiet in church. This restrictive teaching is akin to Quranic legislation. See Colossians 3:18, Ephesians 5:24, I Peter 2:1-6, I Timothy 2:5-12, and I Corinthians 14:34-35.

The Quran and Women: Challenge to Culture

However inadequate these above-mentioned teachings and practices seem to be, they were a significant step forward. Comparatively speaking, against the backdrop of seventh-century Arabia, the Quran was a virtual champion of women's rights. Much of what the Quran advocates for women was not seen in the West until approximately a hundred years ago. Many Muslim women of this century are reclaiming rights and a status given them by the Quran, but whittled away during the last fourteen hundred years. Here is a list of teachings from the Quran to which many Muslims point with pride.

1. Female infanticide was abolished.

2. Primogeniture, when inheritance goes only to the oldest male heir, was banned.

3. Men must pay a dowry to their wives. This money went to the wife, not her father, and it was her private property to do with as she saw fit. Moreover, she was able to keep it even after a divorce.

4. Women could inherit property from husbands and fathers.

5. Women could retain their maiden names.

6. Divorce may be initiated by women according to the Quran after sincere attempts to preserve marriage are made and as a last resort.

7. Husbands must sign marriage contracts to indicate how much they are willing to pay their wives in event of divorce.

8. Pre-nuptial agreements may include conditions set by a wife and they must be honored.

9. Women have final approval on a marriage partner arranged by her parents.

10. Widows have the right to remarry and are encouraged to do so.

11. Religious equality of sexes before God and intellectual equality of men and women in Allah's act of creation: "O Mankind, reverence your Guardian and Lord Who created you from a single Person, created of like nature and from them twain scattered countless men and women" (4:i), and a similar passage in 39:6: "He created you from a single Person; Then created, of like nature, his mate."

There are two verses in the Quran which state the inherent equality before humankind are affirmed. Both have equal access to heaven: "Whosoever does good deeds, whether male or female, while being believers, they shall enter paradise." (4:124, 40:40)

75

The logic of this equality in creation means that "women shall have rights similar to the rights against them according to what is equitable." (2:228) The Quran goes on to say in the same verse that men have a "degree of advantage" over women. This seeming imbalance refers not to superiority, but to functional difference. The husband's obligation to provide economic well-being for his family gives him the right to be in charge (4:34). This was never meant to be exploitative or to result in political advantage for the man. In any case, the Islamic doctrine of *tawhid* is at work here—equality before God implies equality before each other.

12. Muslim men were and are limited to four wives. Polygamy is never encouraged in the Quran. In fact, monogamy is the preferred state and Quranic ideal. The husband is permitted additional wives only on the condition that he is able to treat each wife equally, fairly, and justly, and only if the family, as a unit, will not suffer by the addition of wives (4:3). To prevent exploitation of women and the selfishness of men, the latter may be required to apply for permission before a matrimonial counsel to marry again. So, from the point of view of the Quran, taking a second wife is a solemn agreement to accept certain serious responsibilities. Since it is very difficult to treat each wife impartially, less than 2% of Muslim marriages are polygamous. This means monogamy is the rule.

In early Islam, there was a historic basis and social need for polygamy—to protect the security of surplus women.* A metaphysical basis was soon offered by Muslim scholars to explain polygamy. The Oneness of the Male Principle was joined by a multiplicity of Divine Infinitude in the form of Females. This helped to preserve polygamy as an institution, but the Quranic ideal of monogamy was the final arbiter of how women should fare in marriage.

Islam did provide legal rights for women, especially in the area of family life. Quranic advocacy of women and its correction of the harsh treatment women typically received in the seventh century, contains a strong sense of prophetic justice.

From a western standpoint, the Quran may not outline an even playing field for men and women. When seen from within the society of Islam, however, men and women are less opposites and more complements to the other. The sensitivity of Jane Smith provides fresh insight to a problem endemic to world religions. It is worth quoting in its entirety:

It is my opinion that Western feminists are beginning to recognize what historians of religion were a long time in realizing—that the kinds of assumptions one

*The Roman Catholic Church is facing the same problem today in parts of Africa. Social and economic reasons are forcing the Church to reconsider polygamy as a Christian option. See *Polygamy Reconsidered* by Eugene Hillman, New York: Orbis Press, 1973.

brings to the observation of another culture often lead to the asking of questions basically inappropriate to that culture. We must begin to listen more carefully to what persons from within cultural traditions, in this case particularly women, are saying in response to their own felt needs and priorities. The point has been made repeatedly that the history of women in Islam reveals a clear pattern of male domination. But what I have tried to indicate is that from within the Islamic perspective this is a divinely-initiated and therefore natural and right circumstance. In all religions the rules have been made by men, insist Western feminists, and women must play the parts thus determined for them. But for the Muslim women this is not necessarily the case. Listen again to my Egyptian friend:

> [Western feminists] say that the rules have been made by men for women to follow. But they do not understand that Muslim women believe these to be divine rules.... By liberating them from these 'man-made' regulations they are in fact liberating them from their own religion.[23]

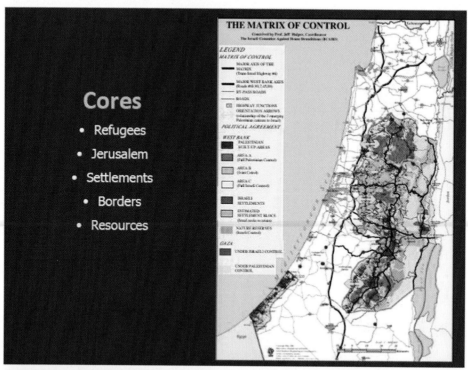

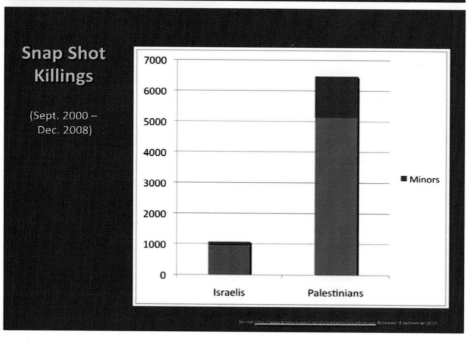

Graphic Novels

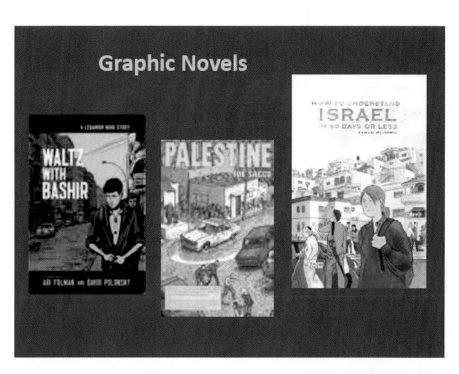

Two State Solution?
July 2005

Cores of the Conflict

- Refugees
- Jerusalem
- Settlements
- Borders
- Resources

US Foreign Policy Starting Points

Values + Power = Achieve Goals

Rhetoric/Reality
- Government by election
- Free market economies
- Individual liberties
- Economic wealth
- Security

Perceived/Actual
- Size of population
- Size of economy
- Military projection
- Progressive agenda
- Education (and system)
- English language

Systemic/Aspirational
1. Stabile government and society among friends
2. Hydrocarbons to reach the world market without shocks
3. Maintain Israel as a hegemon
4. Defeat militant groups using terror tactics organized around self-professed Muslim politics
5. Solidly withdraw from Afghanistan and Iraq
6. Manage Iran's nuclear issue

Newton Public Schools

100 Walnut Street
Newton, MA 02460

Telephone
(617) 559-6100

Fax
(617) 559-6101

Overview of Newton's High School Curriculum
From David Fleishman, Superintendent of Schools

The Newton Public Schools value openness and critical thinking. One of the gifts we give our students is the opportunity to carefully listen to and debate different perspectives. Our children hear opinions and, especially now in the internet age, they are exposed to a multitude of viewpoints. As a result, teaching critical thinking is an increasingly important skill. We can present a range of perspectives, including those that are not widely accepted, and challenge students to examine evidence, debate the issues, and articulate their thoughts. In this way, students gain skills to assess the quality of an argument and the claims that are made.

With regard to the history curriculum in particular, our mission statement calls for students to "appreciate the historical and cultural influences that shape their individual identities, our national identity, and the cultures and countries that share our planet," and to "learn to assess and interpret evidence, to understand change over time, to think logically and express themselves clearly." While much of our material is factual, we also present a range of opinions and perspectives. Our educators work to ensure that students understand when they are receiving a point of view, as opposed to a proven fact. We do not teach students that they should agree with every perspective and point of view they encounter in our classrooms; we are focused on teaching students *how* to think, rather than *what* to think.

The high school curriculum begins with a two-year world history sequence—ninth grade is a survey of World History, covering 300 C.E. to 1775 followed by tenth grade World History, 1775-Present. In eleventh grade the focus is on United States history, pre-civil war to contemporary times with particular attention to the changing role of American political institutions. Grade twelve offers a variety of courses and electives on topics ranging from AP European History, to Comparative Governments, Psychology, Race, Class and Gender, and more.

The ninth grade history curriculum includes a survey of world history in which students begin their studies with the golden ages of empires in Europe, Asia, Africa, and the Americas and continue on to the dawning of the Industrial Age. The ninth grade history curriculum covers the historical origins and basic beliefs of major world religions, including Judaism, Christianity, Islam, Hinduism, and Buddhism. We strive to teach majority and mainstream interpretations of all the religions covered in the ninth grade course, recognizing that all religions have sects and adherents who differ in their interpretations of the faith. Our students learn the origins of each religion and the development of that religion over time; we teach religion from a historical rather than a theological point of view.

Newton Public Schools

100 Walnut Street
Newton, MA 02460

Telephone
(617) 559-6100

Fax
(617) 559-6101

Several questions have been asked recently about our high schools' History curriculum. The following includes these questions and answers.

How do teachers in Newton decide what topics to teach and what materials to use?
The topics of most classes in the Newton Public Schools are determined by the State curriculum frameworks and Newton's own curriculum documents, which are publically available. Course textbooks are chosen and purchased citywide, after a rigorous selection process involving teachers, students, and administrators. Supplemental teaching materials are gathered by teachers working in collaboration with their colleagues and supervisors.

What happens if parents or citizens have concerns about the curriculum?
Questions or concerns about specific elements of the curriculum should be brought to appropriate administrators at the building level. These administrators review the concern, and investigate the issue. The administrator(s) then take whatever actions they consider necessary to ensure quality education for Newton students.

Is this sequence of events typical?
Parents concerns are not frequent, but they do arise. Over the past few years, administrators have reviewed questions about curriculum in all major academic subjects. Sometimes the review results in changes, and sometimes it does not. In all cases, administrators are guided by their professional judgment along with the mission and values of the Newton Public Schools.

What is the "Arab World Studies Notebook" (AWSN), and how was it used in Newton's high schools?
The *Arab World Studies Notebook* is a binder of supplementary teaching resources on Islam, the Islamic Empires of the middle ages and Arab society and culture. It was purchased by the Newton Public Schools in the mid-1990s, at a time when there were very few teaching resources on Islam available. The AWSN included both primary and secondary resources. Some teachers used some of the resources, and others used none.

What happened with the "Arab World Studies Notebook" in Newton's High Schools?
In the fall of 2011, a parent at Newton South raised concerns about one of the readings from a secondary source in the AWSN. The reading was used by a 9th grade teacher during a lesson on women in Islam. The teacher highlighted a controversial statement in the reading and noted that it was a biased perspective. The teacher acted in a manner that is consistent with the way in which faculty teach perspective. After reviewing the reading with the 9th grade teachers, the History Department head decided to remove the reading. As far as we know, this article was not used by any faculty member at Newton North. During the winter, there was a further review of the AWSN and it was decided that it would no longer be used at Newton South. While it included primary sources that were of value to some faculty, there was a general sense that the materials were outdated. By the end of the 2011-2012 school year, a similar decision was made to remove the AWSN at Newton North High School.

Attachment 5: Newton South High School principal's response to a request for curricular materials

May 15, 2012

Hillel Stavis
JointMedia News Service
(617) 823-3420

     Re: *Public Records Request Received 5/8/12*

Dear Mr. Stavis:

In reference to your recent public records request, Newton South High School responds as follows:

> *The lesson plans, weekly plans, outline syllabi and reading*
> *material supplemental to the course textbook(s) relating to the teaching*
> *of world religions and the Arab Israeli conflict*

> *Items such as what students are expected to do for the class*
> *(ie. read certain pages of the text, read handouts, watch a*
> *television program, bring in homework, research particular information,*
> *etc); what the class will cover (ie. topic(s) of discussion, films*
> *viewed, speakers presented, handouts distributed, etc.); homework or*
> *other work assigned during the class (ie. papers, research,*
> *interviews students are assigned to do, etc).*

> *If material is duplicated for more than one teacher, we only*
> *need one copy. If not too burdensome, we would like to see the above material*
> *dating back to the 2010 school year.*

We estimate it will take teachers 5 hours for search and segregation time to review available hard copy and electronic artifacts. As there are 17 teachers who fall under your request, this yields 85 hours. Pursuant to the rules and regulations of the Massachusetts Supervisor of Public Records, the average hourly rate for the lowest paid employee capable of performing the task of segregation – in this case the teachers themselves - is $42.86. Total search costs will therefore be at least $3,643.10. We would then provide hard copies of these documents

at 20 cents per page.

If you wish to proceed with the request for the above e-mails, we will require a check in the amount of $3,643.10 payable to the City of Newton to begin the search and segregation of these documents. We will await word from you on whether or not you wish to proceed with this request.

Very truly yours,

Joel Stembridge
Principal, Newton South High School

Superintendent Responds To Parent Concerns About Middle East Curriculum

By **Admin** - December 8, 2012

By Astha Agarwal and Melanie Erspamer

Superintendent David Fleishman recently issued a statement intending to clarify and bring to conclusion the months-long debate over Newton's use of the Arab World Studies Notebook in high school history classes.

The notebook, a binder of information about Islam and Arab culture, has been used by the Newton schools since the 1990's. Last year, due to questions over its potential bias and outdatedness, it was removed from the curriculum.

Residents have been speaking out on the issue during the public comment period of School Committee meetings throughout the spring and fall.

"[T]eaching critical thinking is an increasingly important skill," Fleishman said in his Nov. 26

statement. "We can present a range of perspectives, including those that are not widely accepted, and challenge students to examine evidence, debate the issues, and articulate their thoughts."

Recent concern over the notebook arose when Shiri Pagliuso, a freshman at the time, was assigned an article from the notebook in history class. The article, titled "Arab Women: An Introduction," discussed the successes and accomplishments of Arab Islamic women.

A particular sentence in the article worried her, though, and she brought it home to her father. It read: "Over the past four decades, women have been active in the Palestinian resistance movement. Several hundred have been imprisoned, tortured, and killed by Israeli occupation forces."

Tony Pagliuso, Shiri's father, was angered by what he saw as strong bias from the notebook against Israel and Jews, and he decided to take action.

"I thought it was outrageous, having lived in Israel myself," Pagliuso said. "It was outright propaganda."

Pagliuso voiced his concern to the history teacher who distributed it in class, History Department Head Jennifer Morrill, and Principal Joel Stembridge. Unsatisfied with their responses, Pagliuso then proceeded to alert Mayor Setti Warren, the Anti-Defamation League New England, and the Israeli Consulate General.

Warren organized a meeting between Pagliuso, Stembridge, Morrill, and the teacher, who was unable to attend. Although Pagliuso said the meeting itself was unsuccessful, shortly after it, the school removed the article and then proceeded to remove the entire notebook.

"We felt that in the case of this article, there was a better way to teach [the Israel-Palestine conflict] because the article was outdated and sloppy," Stembridge said. "That doesn't mean we made a decision about removing the concept. We didn't remove the concepts or the varying perspectives but we felt that in this case this article was not the best to show this complexity."

This is not the first time the notebook had been challenged. Over the years, several schools and institutions across the country have removed it, citing it as a biased source and pointing out that its publishers — the Middle East Policy Council and Arab World and Islamic Resources — are both funded by Saudi Arabia.

Stembridge said that although concern over the notebook was raised at South a few years ago, it did not come to his attention at that time.

Despite these controversial passages, the notebook also included many primary sources, including comparisons of quotations from the Torah, New Testament and Qur'an, which several teachers found helpful for their students.

The notebook, however, was not used as a required part of the curriculum at South. In fact, many teachers never used it.

"[The AWSN] wasn't part of the curriculum," Stembridge said. "It was a supplement. It may seem like a fine point but I think it's an important distinction to make."

Though South stopped using the notebook last winter, North continued using it and in the spring. A similar concern led to its removal from North as well.

"As far as I was concerned, by the winter of last year, we had really thought deeply about these concerns and acted on them," Morrill said. "What I've heard from School Committee meetings is that there is a still a perception that we didn't act on this father's concern, and I'm really sorry to hear that because I think we did."

A group of still-worried parents and citizens kept the discussion ongoing in Newton school committee meetings, until Fleishman released his statement on the issue.

The statement discusses the purpose of school, specifically that its aim is to promote critical thinking in students, contribute to their ability to understand and think about documents containing various perspectives, and teach "how to think, rather than what to think."

The statement goes on to describe the sequence of events that led to the notebook's removal from the Newton schools.

Charles Jacobs, Newton resident and co-founder of Americans for Peace and Tolerance, said he was not pleased with the superintendent's statement.

"I am certain that the school would never consider using a defamatory attack on any other group as an example to use in a "critical thinking" lesson. Would Newton teachers, for example, use KKK racism?" Jacobs said.

"Mr. Pagliuso's daughter, after going through this critical thinking exercise, did not know, nor was she told by her teacher, that this was a defamatory lie used by the enemies of the Jews to harm the Jewish people."

Both Jacobs and School Committee Vice Chair Matt Hills have written about the issue in recent issues of the Newton Tab.

Pagliuso, like Jacobs, said he believes that this material should never have even been introduced into the school system. "I am not an activist," Pagliuso said. "That was not part of this. I was just shocked at reading this article."

Although the teacher presented the notebook as a biased source and conveyed that the article's main focus was Arab women, Pagliuso and Jacobs said that the only use for such material would be as an example of propaganda.

"This is high school and these are malleable minds; there are still some kids who come away taking that [belief] with them [at face value]," Pagliuso said. "I would be just as equally upset with propaganda against Arabs. I wouldn't accept any form of propaganda armed at any religious or ethnic group."

Some students, however, feel that exposure to different, even extreme, perspectives is important for students. Sophomore Jack Rabinovitch thinks that students should read this type of propaganda in their history classes and learn to make judgments from there.

"I think the best way to make kids learn is to give them even the most radical perspective," Rabinovitch said. "I think parents sullying that variance don't believe their children can make choices for themselves."

Even now, the issue of how much transparency the Newton schools should offer to parents and citizens who want to influence the curriculum continues to be disputed.

"I would not be in favor of asking teachers to vet supplementary documents they want with an outside board," Stembridge said.

There have been other concerns in the past over both curricular and supplementary documents. One parent proposed the removal of the Old Testament, a request that was not granted.

Morrill said she encourages parents to voice their concerns, and she believes it is her responsibility to take them seriously.

"I think that if a parent has a concern about a document or anything that their child has been given, that they should ask," Morrill said. "If...they think something is not working despite our best efforts, we need to talk about it."

Morrill said she is proud of South's teachers for making an effort to teach the Israeli-Palestinian conflict despite the controversy that surrounds it.

"There are many schools that don't teach this conflict, because it's hard to teach it well," Morrill said. "We believe we should teach it because it's so important. We take the privilege of being teachers so very seriously, and we know that we have to be very careful to do it well."

Morrill said she is satisfied with the Newton Public Schools' response to the parents' concerns regarding the Arab World Studies Notebook.

"I do think this is an example of the system working well," Morrill said. "We had a father who had a concern, we looked at his concern…we agreed with his concern and we acted.

"In the end, I think it did work well, and it saddens me that people think it didn't work well."

Letters *to the* Editor

Write to: The Editor, The Jewish Advocate,
15 School St., Boston, MA 02108
E-mail: editorial@thejewishadvocate.com • Fax: 617-367-9310

JCRC seeks Newton parents' input and schools transparency

We at JCRC are deeply disappointed by the most recent ad from Americans for Peace and Tolerance (APT) in this paper (on Feb. 7) attacking the ADL for its leadership on behalf of our community while offering new allegations of anti-Israel bias in Newton public school classrooms.

How Israel is presented in American education systems is a challenge that requires sober analysis and serious conversations with school officials in districts around the nation. Continued assaults on ADL do nothing to address this challenge while unfairly demeaning an organization that has a venerable and noble record of combatting hate and bias for over 100 years. Intra-communal sniping and accusations are a distraction and a detriment to facing our most critical challenges as a united community.

The latest ad presents excerpts of teaching materials allegedly used in the classroom. We at JCRC have communicated to APT repeatedly and as recently as last week that absent a firsthand account from parents of students in the Newton school district who can provide us with the actual classroom materials their children were given, the information as presented in this ad does not provide a basis for reopening our inquiry into classroom materials in the Newton school curriculum.

Of course, the question of what biases our children may be taught in school is of great importance and we continue to welcome the opportunity to meet any Newton parent whose child has brought home objectionable materials. If presented with direct reports from Newton district parents of said materials, JCRC would, without hesitation, reopen our discussion with school district leaders.

Please be assured that we will protect the confidentiality of any parent who so wishes. Please write us at info@jcrcboston.org, mentioning "Newton Schools" in the subject line.

Though JCRC is not prepared to provide validation to the new allegations at this time, we would suggest that the Newton School Committee – as an elected body representing the voters of Newton – could put this entire chapter to rest by publicly addressing the ongoing allegations once and for all. While the school system shouldn't be required to respond to innuendo and unsubstantiated allegations, it would benefit the entire community if they would provide a public accounting about how curriculum is developed and how and where materials are approved for classroom distribution. In the light of such transparency, we would all feel more comforted by their public assurances regarding this matter.

JEREMY BURTON,
Executive Director
JILL GOLDENBERG,
President
JCRC of Greater Boston

THE JEWISH ADVOCATE MAY 23, 2014

Learning some hard lessons about Newton's curriculum

New information has surfaced regarding the Newton Public School controversy. Compelled to comply with state law, the school's administrators recently were forced to release an initial batch of 9th- and 10th-grade history lesson plans used to teach about the Middle East.

Most of the information, initially withheld from the public despite requests from parents, taxpayers and even a Newton alderman, was delivered to Americans for Peace and Tolerance (APT's) offices in response to a public records request. Once our request is completed, we will post the records at opennewton-schools.org. Newton citizens, especially those who are Jewish, will not be pleased.

For two years, we have been told by Superintendent David Fleishman and others that the Arab World Studies Notebook (ASWN) was removed from all classrooms and has not been used to teach Newton students since 2011. But the official documents we received show that Newton South High School assigned readings from

Charles Jacobs

Ilya Feoktistov

the AWSN to 9th-grade students in at least three separate classes in the last school year – months after claims that it was "eliminated."

The AWSN has been condemned by the American Jewish Committee (AJC) as a fraudulent anti-Israel text created by Saudi-funded organizations. After a parent complaint about the AWSN was rebuffed in 2011, grassroots Jewish groups lobbied for more than a year until the schools claimed to remove it. But school documents now show that the AWSN continues to be taught. We are not sure if this is a matter of integrity or incompetence.

Apart from the Saudi hate-lesson, the materials released validate our claims that Newton South educates students to adopt anti-Israel viewpoints through the use of biased textbooks, readings, maps and people, academic exercises. Until now, our knowledge of what Newton students are being taught was limited to what we received from students in only a few of classes. We now know that almost all the teachers in Newton South teach from the same problematic anti-Israel materials we saw previously.

The teachers' class notes we received directly contradict Newton school officials' claims that any anti-Israel materials are balanced by pro-Israel materials. For example, school

administrators claimed that a series of assigned maps (created by a Palestine Liberation Organization propaganda unit, but never identified as such) were balanced by maps with a pro-Israel viewpoint. No such maps can be found. Several maps show Palestinian refugee dispersal and camp locations but there is no map showing the expulsion of Jews from Arab lands.

Several Newton teachers use a textbook written by James Gelvin, an anti-Israel ideologue and a pioneer of the academic boycott against Israel. Gelvin wrote the textbook while receiving payments from Sheikh Zayed, the anti-Semitic Emirates billionaire whose $2 million gift Boston's Jewish heroine, Rachel Fish, forced Harvard University to reject because of the anti-Semitism of his "think tank."

In Newton schools, students are given an assignment called POV, which purports to show the Israeli and Palestinian "points of view" on various events in the history of the conflict. Yet these points of view are often either blatantly or subtly anti-Israel.

Centuries of Islamic religious teaching that Jews are to be a subjugated people, not permitted self-rule, are erased from Newton's "history" lessons. To ensure that students won't see Judeophobia as a root cause of the conflict, they are given a doctored, whitewashed version of the Hamas

Charter from which the terror group's genocidal anti-Jewish pronouncements are removed so that the jihadist murderers can be falsely portrayed as mere militant nationalists.

Newton officials have sought to deflect accusations they permit biased instruction by saying that it's not anti-Israel but only an exercise in "critical thinking." ("We don't teach students what to think, but how to think," Fleishman says.) Newton teachers' class notes tell a different story. Just as with the cleansed Hamas Charter, one teacher insists that the Arab war against Israel "is *not* inherently a religious conflict. *This is a comflict over land*." (Emphasis hers.) Many Middle East scholars would disagree, so why not let students decide for themselves? Newton students, the documents show, are made to debate whether the Jews have a right to a homeland of their own, but are never asked to ponder if any other people, such as the Palestinians themselves, deserve a state.

"Critical thinking" is increasingly being used throughout our nation to to justify teaching hatred and the demonization of Jews. But is there a public school anywhere in America where students receive critical thinking lessons about Islamist honor killings, female genital mutilation, the enslavement and forced conversion of infidel women, or today's forced exodus and slaughter of Christians from the Middle East? It's doubtful. These topics are made taboo, they don't fit the anti-Western, anti-Judeo-

Christian narrative that permeates our schools.

A week or so before we received the public records from Newton, 478 high school students from Newton signed a letter defending "the history department in the face of allegations by [APT] that Newton's Middle East curriculum is anti-Israel." It was published in The Jewish Advocate and The Newton Tab.

One suspects, from both the language and content of the letter (posted on APT's website) that it was not written by students alone. People can judge for themselves.

Ironically, students who parrot their teachers are expressing an image opposite of the one young people like to present that of cool, independent-minded, even rebellious youth. How were they herded into a pack of 478 conformists? What happened to the courage to, in the words of their generation's bumper sticker, "question authority?"

It takes no courage to whine about Israel – Jews won't beat you up. Bravery today would be to stand up for black slaves in Sudan and Nigeria, abused and oppressed women under Islamic rule, Sharia-compliant hanging of gays. Sadly, the most these victims will likely get from today's students (and our nation's leaders) is hashtag activism.

Charles Jacobs is president and Ilya Feoktistov is research director of Americans for Peace and Tolerance (peaceand-tolerance.org).

Attachment 10: Letter to the Editor by Russel Pergament

THE JEWISH ADVOCATE   APRIL 22, 2016

LETTERS TO THE EDITOR

Cowardice in Newton

Newton was rocked recently by a confrontation between Jewish parents and others enraged that already discredited school Superintendent David Fleishman decided to keep a series of anti-Semitic incidents in the city's schools secret from the public.

For months, "Burn the Jews" graffiti on school walls and swastikas carved into snowbanks were ignored system-wide, up to Mayor Setti Warren's office. Evidently, the ambitious pol concluded it was not politically expedient to acknowledge the extensive anti-Semitic activity within his schools. Warren called a public meeting, presumably to discuss this; rather than deal with the hate crimes, though, Warren subjected the increasingly restive crowd to his mother-in-law's life story. He virtually ignored the Jewish families' concerns as he attempted to package the evening as a blueprint for Newton's next century of "inclusiveness and diversity."

Coverage varied. The redoubtable The Jewish Advocate headlined page one with, "Newton avoids addressing anti-Semitic incidents." The Newton TAB wrote, "Newton forum on prejudice gets rowdy." The Boston Globe ran, "Jewish leaders decry 'disrespect' at meeting" or what some have re-tagged, "Jews behaving badly." Anyone who spends 2:19 viewing video of the meeting will conclude there was no heckling or disrespect. One can only speculate on why the Globe gave this falsehood such prominent play.

Entrenched municipal bureaucracies resent citizens who challenge their way of doing business. Sometimes people have to act to protect themselves, or in this case, their children. In Newton, they have put City Hall on notice. Things must change.

RUSSEL PERGAMENT
Publisher, MASSterList

Attachment 11: Syllabus for 2015 for the Israeli/Palestinian conflict at Newton South High School

Name: _____

Unit SIX: Towards a Two State Solution: The Israeli / Palestinian Conflict (1917-present)

Essential Unit Questions
- Historically, what factors have aggravated the relationship between Israelis and Arabs? What factors have allowed for negotiation, peace, and co-existence?
- In regards to the Israeli/Palestinian conflict today, what are the most viable prospects for peace and the most serious concerns for conflict?

Day One: An Introduction to the Israeli/Palestinian Conflict (from 1917-2000)
Due:
Reading: History of the Israeli-Palestinian Conflict by Negar Katirai (Council on Foreign Relations) and Dr. Mark LeVine (University of California-Irvine) [via PBS]
Questions:
- Based on your understanding of the reading, identify what you believe are the 6 most important dates – events that were major turning points or significant occurrences that define the conflict.
- Based on your understanding of the reading, identify 3 historical conflicts you believe are still relevant to the conflict between Israelis and Palestinians today. Why?
- Based on your understanding of the reading, identify 3 examples that illustrate negotiation and compromise can happen in this conflict.
- Based on your understanding of the reading, identify 3 events that may have stoked past resentments between the two sides but may no longer be relevant to Israelis and Palestinians living today.

Day Two: An Introduction to the Key Issues in the Peace Process (from 1967-2013)
Due:
Video: Challenges in Defining an Israeli-Palestinian Border (via the nytimes.com)
Watch: Part 1, Part 2, and Part 3 on the interactive website. Look at the pictures below for each section.
Questions:
- Based on the video: In defining a permanent border between an Israeli state and a proposed Palestinian state . . .
  o . . . what do you think are the top 5 concerns Israelis have about defining a new border.
  o . . . what do you think are the top 5 concerns Palestinians have about defining a new border.
- In the video, not all Israelis share the same opinions on where a border gets drawn. Brainstorm 2-3 factors that might contribute to this. Why do you think the Palestinians interviewed tend to express a more unified opinion?

Day Three: An Introduction to the Key Issues in the Peace Process (from 1967-2013) (pt. 2)
Due:
Video: Challenges in Defining an Israeli-Palestinian Border (via the nytimes.com)
Watch: Part 4 and Part 5 on the interactive website. Look at the pictures below for each section.
Questions: Add to the materials you gathered during your last homework assignment.
- Based on the video: In defining a permanent border between an Israeli state and a proposed Palestinian state . . .
  o . . . what do you think are additional concerns Israelis have about defining a new border.
  o . . . what do you think are additional concerns Palestinians have about defining a new border.
- In the video, not all Israelis share the same opinions on where a border gets drawn. Brainstorm 2-3 factors that might contribute to this. Why do you think the Palestinians interviewed tend to express a more unified opinion?

Up Next: *The Final Project*

93

Day Four: What would a Two-State Solution look like? (1994-present)

Due:

Task: Based on the character you receive, complete the "Two-State Solution" worksheet you receive in class. Complete the blank map and the attached questionnaire.

Web Resources:

- Crisis Guide: The Israeli-Palestinian Conflict (Chapter II: The Territorial Puzzle) [via the Council on Foreign Relations] – *This website provides both graphics and narration on key issues in relationship to geography in the conflict. The Regional Complexities section is particularly helpful for this assignment.*
- Is Peace Possible? Two State Solution Simulator [via The S. Daniel Abraham Center for Middle East Peace & The Atlantic] – *This website identifies the key demands of both sides and offers you the ability to adjust the current borders of Israel in accordance with establish peace plan proposals. You do not need to complete a map on this site, but it may be helpful to play around with the simulator to generate some ideas for your worksheet.*

Day Five: What would a Two-State Solution look like? (1994-present) - Part II

Due:

Task: Write a 1-2 page reflection that covers the following points and submit via email by the beginning of your respective class. (Worth 30 points – utilize unit vocabulary and concepts / no thesis necessary)

- What evidence did the simulation and the overall unit provide that illustrates a two-state solution is viable?
- What evidence did the simulation and the overall unit provide that illustrates a two-state solution is unlikely in the foreseeable future?
- What was the single most important thing you took away from the simulation and the unit overall?

Israeli/Palestinian Conflict:
-Peace Plan Simulation – from the Bottom Up-

Summary
This activity asks you to consider how a variety of people would respond to new rounds of negotiations between the Israeli government and the Palestinian Authority. Several years ago, the New York Times interviewed a variety of people living in Israel and the Palestinian Territories to get their opinions on a variety of negotiable issues. You will assigned to one of these people for our simulation. Using the available video footage and the information we have studied in class, imagine you have been assigned by the US State Department to interview one person and report back on their thoughts regarding the peace process.

Based on the available information, you may have to infer a good deal about what your character would propose. You may not be able to answer all of the sections of the questionnaire below. This is fine. This activity acknowledges that average Israelis and Palestinians may not have a fully formulated opinion on all facets of the peace plan. That said, based on the evidence available, you should be able to surmise a fairly complete submission.

One State / Two State / Three State
Most students will likely submit a map proposal that contains two states: Israel and a future Palestine. That said, some of the characters hold views that suggest support for a One State Solution. The One State Solution, when it is argued for, often comes in three very different forms:

- a secular multi-ethnic state with equal legal and political rights for Israelis and Palestinians
- a Greater Israel that annexes much of the West Bank and resettles Palestinians in neighboring Arab nations
- an Islamist Palestine that includes all of Gaza, the West Bank, and present day Israel

There has also been some limited discussion of a three state solution:

- Israel's border return to pre-67 lines, the West Bank becomes the recognized Palestinian State, and Gaza is left to develop as a separate, independent nation under currently undefined terms.

Additional Resources
- Three Options for Peace by David Makovsky (2011 – New York Times): With roughly 4% of the Israeli population living in settlements within the West Bank, some have asked how a viable Palestinian state can be created while respecting the land claims of the settlers. Although some believe these settlers will have to return to Israel, others (including President Obama) believe that calculated "land swaps" between Israel and a future Palestine could offer a viable solution. Here are three proposals from the last round of failed negotiations in 2008.
- Crisis Guide: The Israeli / Palestinian Conflict (Council on Foreign Relations): Chapter II: The Territorial Puzzle offers a one-stop resource to understanding relevant issues related to geography and borders. You can watch this in its entirety or skip to sections you need to review. Each section has a short narration that outlines the major issues.
- Is Peace Possible? Two State Solution Simulator (The Atlantic and the S. Daniel Abraham Center for Middle East Peace): If you already feel like you have a good grasp on the core issues and want to a more advanced tool for redrawing the borders of Israel and a future Palestine, this web app offers a very powerful engine for exploring land swap options.

Characters (see *Challenges in Defining an Israeli / Palestinian border* website on nytimes.com)

Mahdi Abdul Hadi	Sima Halif	Dr. Boaz Ganor	Hala Jahshan
Uri Segal	Najla Kayed	Ibrahim Jabr	Yuli Edelstein
Adalia Danielle	Nawaf Zagarneh	Dimitri Kabanov	Shaul Arieli
Salomaa	Idan Ben-Ari	Jamal Abu	Nabil Shaath
Marco Carmignani	Uzi Sharbaf	Khamseh	Abed Kassab
(UN)	Murad Abu Shafi	Gilad Ben David	

Attachment 12: Teacher's class notes for 10th grade unit on Israeli-Palestinian conflict in 2013

CLASS NOTES FOR ISRAEL PALISTINE (STUDENT & TEACHER DISCUSSION)

Towards a Two State Solution: The Israeli / Palestinian Conflict (1917-2013)

May 1st, 2013
Introduction to the Unit

1. **What do we (think we) know** about the conflict? [strictly 5 minutes]
2. **A note on teaching controversial topics...**
3. **Two themes to begin considering ...**

- The Israeli / Palestinian Conflict is **not** entirely unique in the world

    o **Jewish nationalism (Zionism)** and **Palestinian nationalism** seek essentially the same goal: a state that can provide security, economic opportunity, and *a connection to a land that is of significant historical, cultural, and religious significance.* This is consistent with many other forms of **nationalism** around the world.
    o This violent conflict is not unique either - there are many **multi-ethnic states** around the world where tensions arise <u>over control of land</u>.
    o Although religion is an important factor in defining elements of the conflict, I would assert this is **not** inherently a religious conflict. <u>This is a conflict over land.</u>

- People defined by tragedy (this may help us understand the conflict's intractability)

    o For the **Jewish diaspora** and Jewish Israelis, the Holocaust is considered a major turning point in Jewish history. The phrase **"never again"** captures the attitude that Jews needed to defend themselves in a manner unprecedented in the history of that ethnic group - and that a strong **Jewish state** is the only mechanism that can provide for this.
    o For the **Palestinian diaspora** and Palestinians living in the Occupied Territories, Israeli takeover of Palestinian land (first in 1947-48 war and then to a greater extent after the 1967 war) is considered a great national tragedy. The history of prolonged resistance, whether violent or nonviolent, is rooted in this aspiration to establish a Palestinian state in land historically owned and farmed by Palestinians.

4. **Begin reading homework** (since many of you are still working on your papers)

Key Dates and Turning Points in the Israeli/Palestinian Conflict

1. **Crowd source a timeline:**
   - What were the events that stood out to you last night? Lets gather as many as we can.
   - You each have **3 votes** to utilize - put a check underneath the dates you think are the most important. You can place three checks under one date, one under three, etc...
   - Any event receiving *more than* 8 votes will be discussed in the next round.
   - While you are voting, please identify any names or terms you didn't understand in the reading and place them in the I want to know more about... column.

2. **Discussing our timeline:**
   - What is significant about the dates we've identified?
   - Based on the other questions you had to answer last night, **what general conclusions** can we draw regarding the dates we've identified?
     - *We saw situations where countries are weary of balance of power - and some peace treaties actually escalate a violent response.*
     - *A lot of the time Israel is trying more for peace - and to give up things up to achieve peace - is this a viable analysis? Israel also controls the land - they have something to give... Palestinians have less to give in this situation.*
     - *Are the peace-treaties in Israel's favor or are they in the favor of peace.*

3. **Previewing Tonight's Homework**
   - To understand the history of the peace process, we need to understand the core issues at stake in any future resolution of the conflict. In **1995**, negotiations between Israelis and Palestinians yielded the following **5 points** as central to any future peace plan:
     - **Secure borders** that provide both safety and mobility for both sides must be established.
     - Palestinians maintain that all **refugees** (a broad term for Palestinians living inside and outside the Occupied Territories) are given enough land to accommodate their population's economic needs and human rights.
     - The question of who will control Israeli **settlement** communities in the West Bank must be resolved.
     - Both Israelis and Palestinians want access to adequate **water resources** along the Jordan River and the Mediterranean Sea.

The question of who will control the city of **Jerusalem**, significant for religious, cultural, and economic reasons, must be resolved.

May 3, 2013
Issues in Finding a Two State Solution

1. **Review Video Content**
2. **Questions from Last Night**
   - **What are the top 5+ issues that Israelis see in where a border gets drawn?**

- o Jerusalem is of great importance to the Jewish people and the Jewish faith
- o Boundaries are key to security... Israelis want strong security to stop militants from moving into Israel
- o Israel needs defensible borders and defendable territory
- o Israel wants peace and stability in the region - which leads to security.
- o Resources... water!
- o The settlements in the West Bank are extremely difficult to move: 400,000 people, its difficult to remove these people from their homes, and many of these people are STAUNCHLY opposed to moving.
- o There are a long chunk of people that just don't recognize the other side's right to a state.
- o In terms of arable land - it is in limited supply - how do you evenly distribute arable land.
- o Israelis want to have some control over a future Palestine's borders to prevent a weapons trade and increase in extremism in the Palestinian territories - the experience in Gaza has shaped this cautious approach.

- **What are the top 5 issues that Palestinians see in where a border gets drawn?**
  - o Jerusalem is of great importance to the Islamic faith and Muslim Palestinians
  - o Resources...water!
  - o Economic opportunity needs to increase - Palestinians need access to arable farmland, to urban areas, to transportation networks...
  - o The Palestinians want to see the security wall come down - it not only stifles their movement but it is a symbol of the conflict.
  - o Palestinians believe settlements and the wall are part of a larger effort of Israelis to take all of the West Bank... they fear they will lose the foundation of a future state.
  - o There are a long chunk of people that just don't recognize the other side's right to a state.
  - o In terms of arable land - it is in limited supply - how do you evenly distribute arable land - especially when Israelis have developed more of the irrigation technology.
  - o Palestinians want land and water access to other Arab nations for trade and transportation...
  - o Once (if) Palestine is independent - it has to be fully independent, Israel cannot interfere in the sovereignty of that nation.

- **Why do you think Israelis tend to voice more diverse views on the border issue in comparison to Palestinians?**
  - o With the Palestinians, there is almost universal anxiety in regards to settlements - which in the West Bank, you have direct contact with. Israelis often live quite far away from the W. Bank - and have little contact with the Palestinians.
  - o The Palestinians have a single goal: gain land for a state - on the other hand, the future of Israel could go a lot of different ways - more settlements, less settlements, two states, one states...
  - o It is easier to come a decision to what you want to take - whereas there is more debate on what you want to give.

Attachment 13: POV Timeline

A Modified PROMISES • TIMELINE December 2001

Assignment Part One:
- **For homework:** Read the timeline and highlight the following in the colors you choose:
  o Highlight important leaders in _____
  o Highlight important places in _____
  o Highlight other important information in _____
- **In class:** After highlighting the reading, go back and put stars by the 10 most important events

HISTORY OF THE ISRAELI-PALESTINIAN CONFLICT

The history of the Palestinian-Israeli conflict changes dramatically depending on who is telling it and where they start the story. Therefore, it is important to note that a historic timeline of events concerning this conflict is always difficult to present in an objective manner. For this reason, certain events of the timeline include both a Palestinian (on the right side) and an Israeli (on the left side) perspective.

Zionist movement: *A response to the worsening persecution of European Jews and out of the desire to join the community European countries. Thousands of Jews began immigrating to Palestine, which was then part of the Ottoman Empire.*

BLUE = Israeli Perspective	**GREEN = Palestinian Perspective**
1917	*1915*
The British government, in the Balfour Declaration, stated its support for "the establishment in Palestine of a National Home for the Jewish people."	*Exchange of ten letters between:*
Motivation:	*Britain's high commissioner in Egypt* / *Emir of Mecca and King of the Arabs*
• *sympathy for the Zionist cause*	• *Britain pledged to support Arab independence if Hussein's forces revolted against the Ottomans.*
• *rally Jews to the side of the Allies*	
• *"self determination of small nations"*	• *Hussein envisioned a unified Arab state stretching from Syria to Yemen.*
• *securing British influence of the region east of the Suez Canal*	

1918
As a result of World War I, Britain wins control over the area of Palestine from the Ottoman Empire. The area becomes known as British-mandate Palestine. [A mandate is an authorization to govern over conquered territory]. From 1918 to 1948, Britain governs over the Jews and Arabs living in this territory.

1921
Britain creates TransJordan (now Jordan). First major episode of violence erupts on May Day, leaving scores of Jews and Arabs dead.

Jews described the violence as a "pogrom" or "riots."	Palestinians term the violence a "revolt."

1929
Second major episode of violence spreads throughout the country. Sixty-seven Jews are killed.

1936
In response to killing of a Muslim leader by the British

Arab residents of British Mandate Palestine begin "rioting," causing violence, and the seizure of a shipment of illegal arms destined for the Jewish defense force. The "rioting" lasts until 1939, when the British, in part to obtain Arab support for the recently erupted war with Germany, ban most land sales to Jews.	*Arab residents of British Mandate Palestine begin the "**Great Arab Revolt**," causing violence, and the seizure of a shipment of illegal arms destined for the Jewish defense force. The "revolt" lasts until 1939, when the British, in part to obtain Arab support for the recently erupted war with Germany, ban most land sales to Jews.*

November 1947

The United Nations' General Assembly recommended the partition of British-mandate Palestine into two separate states, one for Jews and one for Arabs. Fighting breaks out soon thereafter, as all the surrounding Arab states rejected the partition plan.

Zionist leaders accepted the proposed partition for tactical and strategic reasons.	*Palestinians considered the proposal unrepresentative of the demographic distribution of Jews and Arabs living in Palestine at that time, and so rejected it.*

1948

Zionist leaders proclaimed the state of Israel. <u>Fighting breaks out between the state of Israel and its Arab neighbors</u> as British troops are leaving the country.

War known by Israelis as "War of Independence"	*War known by Palestinians as "the Catastrophe"*
• *Some 700,000 Palestinians leave what had been British-mandate Palestine.* • *Israel gains control overlarge tracts of land, including some five hundred Palestinian villages.*	• *Some 700,000 Palestinians flee or are driven from what had been British-mandate Palestine.* • *Israel annexes large tracts of land and destroys some five hundred Palestinian villages.*

- Jordan establishes control over the West Bank
- Egypt establishes control of the Gaza Strip.
- Control of Jerusalem is split between Israel in the west and Jordan in the east

December: UN General Assembly passes <u>Resolution 194</u>: Palestinian refugees who wish to return to their homes should be permitted to do so and that those who do not wish to return should be compensated by the state of Israel.

May 1964

422 Palestinian national figures meet in Jerusalem. Creates the Palestine Liberation Organization (PLO), Palestine National Council (PNC), the National Fund and the Palestine Liberation Army (PLA). The meeting also approved a Palestinian national covenant and basic law.

June 1967

Israel gains control over territory formerly controlled by Egypt, Syria and Jordan
- Sinai Peninsula and Gaza Strip from Egypt
- Golan Heights from Syria
- West Bank and East Jerusalem from Jordan.

Israelis call the "Six Day War"	*Palestinians call it: "al-Naksah," or "the Setback."*
• *Israel conducts pre-emptive attack against Egypt* • *Nearly triples size of their territory* • *Rightwing Israelis refer to West Bank and East Jerusalem by the biblical names "Judea and Samaria" and consider the biblical lands of the Jewish people.*	• *Palestinians view this as a violation of international law regarding territory seized during war.* • *Iraq sends forces into Jordan to support the war, even though Jordan had not requested such action.* • *The PLO moves its operations from the West Bank to Jordan.*

In response to the war, the UN Security Council passes <u>Resolution 242,</u> which calls for the
- "withdrawal of Israeli armed forces from territories occupied in the recent conflict [in official UN languages this implies that Israel has to return all the conquered territory];
- termination of all claims or states of belligerency
- respect for and acknowledgement of the sovereignty, territorial integrity and political independence of every state in the area and their right to live in peace within secure and recognized boundaries free from threats or acts of force."

This resolution, with its formula of "land for peace," is the basis of for all subsequent peace negotiations between Israel, Palestinians, and the surrounding Arab states.

September 1970
Through a battle that results in the loss of 3,000 lives, The PLO is forced by Jordan's King Hussein to move headquarters to Lebanon. Arab League and by Gamel Abdel Nasser, leader of Egypt broker the peace agreement.

September 1972
Palestinian gunmen kill 11 Israeli athletes at the Munich Olympics.

October 1973
Egypt and Syria organize a surprise attack on Israeli forces in the Sinai Peninsula and the Golan Heights on the day of the Jewish fast of Yom Kippur and the Muslim month of Ramadan, in which the annual fast is performed. The war lasted for 3 weeks

Israelis = Yom Kippur war.	Arabs = Ramadan war.
Israel saw the war as a military victory because it maintained possession of the Sinai Peninsula and the Golan Heights.	In a surprise attack, Egypt and Syria made initial gains but retreated after Israeli counter-attacks. War was a political victory for Egypt and Syria. Though they overextended their forces and did not succeed in regaining control over the Sinai Peninsula and Golan Heights, Israel's military vulnerabilities were exposed, particularly because the U.S. air-lifted a large supply of weapons to Israel, without which Israel might not have been as successful in defending its territory.

The UN Security Council passes Resolution 338, which calls for an immediate cease-fire and the immediate commencement of negotiations toward the implementation of UNSCR 242 with the goal of "establishing a just and durable peace in the Middle East."

1974
The Arab League declares the PLO the sole spokesman for the Palestinian Arabs.

July 1976
Israeli commandos rescue 98 Israeli and Jewish hostages in Entebbe, Uganda, held by Palestinians who hijacked an Air France Airbus.

1978–1981
President Anwar Sadat of Egypt, Prime Minister Menachem Begin of Israel and President Jimmy Carter of the United States sign the **Camp David accords**.
- Israel agrees to hand back the Sinai Peninsula to Egypt in return for peace and normalization. First time an Arab country signed a peace treaty with Israel thus accepting the state's existence.
- Signing the Camp David accord made Sadat unpopular among many Egyptians as well as Arabs living outside Egypt.
- Egypt is expelled from the Arab League as a reaction to the peace agreement with Israel. Yet in 1980, Egypt and Israel establish diplomatic relations. This led directly to the assassination of Sadat on October 6, 1981, by 3 soldiers of the Egyptian Army.

June 1982
Israel invades Lebanon and establishes a "security zone" in Southern Lebanon in order to block Hezbollah (a Lebanese Shi'a Muslim group whose name means "Party of God" in Arabic) forces from staging attacks on Northern Israeli communities from Lebanon. The Israeli Army reaches Beirut and succeeds in driving out Yasser Arafat's PLO. Arafat moves his organization to Tunisia.

This resolution, with its formula of "land for peace," is the basis of for all subsequent peace negotiations between Israel, Palestinians, and the surrounding Arab states.

September 1970
Through a battle that results in the loss of 3,000 lives, The PLO is forced by Jordan's King Hussein to move headquarters to Lebanon. Arab League and by Gamel Abdel Nasser, leader of Egypt broker the peace agreement.

September 1972
Palestinian gunmen kill 11 Israeli athletes at the Munich Olympics.

October 1973
Egypt and Syria organize a surprise attack on Israeli forces in the Sinai Peninsula and the Golan Heights on the day of the Jewish fast of Yom Kippur and the Muslim month of Ramadan, in which the annual fast is performed. The war lasted for 3 weeks

Israelis = Yom Kippur war.	*Arabs = Ramadan war.*
Israel saw the war as a military victory because it maintained possession of the Sinai Peninsula and the Golan Heights.	*In a surprise attack, Egypt and Syria made initial gains but retreated after Israeli counter-attacks. War was a political victory for Egypt and Syria. Though they overextended their forces and did not succeed in regaining control over the Sinai Peninsula and Golan Heights, Israel's military vulnerabilities were exposed, particularly because the U.S. air-lifted a large supply of weapons to Israel, without which Israel might not have been as successful in defending its territory.*

The UN Security Council passes <u>Resolution 338,</u> which calls for an immediate cease-fire and the immediate commencement of negotiations toward the implementation of UNSCR 242 with the goal of "establishing a just and durable peace in the Middle East."

1974
The Arab League declares the PLO the sole spokesman for the Palestinian Arabs.

July 1976
Israeli commandos rescue 98 Israeli and Jewish hostages in Entebbe, Uganda, held by Palestinians who hijacked an Air France Airbus.

1978–1981
President Anwar Sadat of Egypt, Prime Minister Menachem Begin of Israel and President Jimmy Carter of the United States sign the **Camp David accords**.
- Israel agrees to hand back the Sinai Peninsula to Egypt in return for peace and normalization. First time an Arab country signed a peace treaty with Israel thus accepting the state's existence.
- Signing the Camp David accord made Sadat unpopular among many Egyptians as well as Arabs living outside Egypt.
- Egypt is expelled from the Arab League as a reaction to the peace agreement with Israel. Yet in 1980, Egypt and Israel establish diplomatic relations. This led directly to the assassination of Sadat on October 6, 1981, by 3 soldiers of the Egyptian Army.

June 1982
Israel invades Lebanon and establishes a "security zone" in Southern Lebanon in order to block Hezbollah (a Lebanese Shi'a Muslim group whose name means "Party of God" in Arabic) forces from staging attacks on Northern Israeli communities from Lebanon. The Israeli Army reaches Beirut and succeeds in driving out Yasser Arafat's PLO. Arafat moves his organization to Tunisia.

September 1982

Israel-allied Christian militias enter the Sabra and Shatila refugee camps (housing Palestinian refugees) in Beirut and massacre about 2,000 unarmed Palestinians after PLO fighters are forced out of Lebanon by Israel. The Israeli army occupied the camps at the time. *Official Israeli inquiry found Defense Minister Ariel Sharon indirectly responsible for the killings*

1983–1985

Israel makes a phased withdrawal from most of Lebanon, except for a "security zone" in south.

December 1987

A Palestinian Intifada ["uprising" in Arabic] begins in the West Bank and Gaza. A protest of continued Israeli occupation of the West Bank and Gaza.

Israel tried to suppress the "riots" and "disturbances," with police and army forces, curfews, closing of universities, arrests, deportations and restrictions on economical activities. But a united Palestinian public continued its protests and demonstrations for six years. Some believe that as a result of the Intifada, Israeli public opinion changed and the majority of Israelis became in favor of entering into peace negotiations with the Palestinians. More than 20,000 people were killed or injured between 1987 and 1993.	*Involved demonstrations, strikes, riots and violence. The most symbolically important act of the Intifada was the stoning of Israeli security forces and civilians, often performed by young men and boys. What made the Intifada stand out from earlier forms of protests was its duration and its wide public support, including women. The Intifada also marked the first time that Palestinians living in the West Bank and Gaza became significantly involved in the movement against Israeli occupation. Until then, most of the opposition was organized from outside the occupied territories by the PLO.*

December 1988

Palestinian leader Yasser Arafat condemns all forms of terrorism and recognizes the state of Israel. U.S. President Ronald Reagan authorizes the U.S. to enter into a "substantive dialogue" with the PLO. Israel remains hostile to the PLO. Jordan renounces all territorial claims to the West Bank. The next day, in a clear show of support for the PLO, the UN General Assembly passed Resolution 53/196, which "reaffirmed the inalienable rights of" Palestinians and Syrians in the Golan, called on Israel not to exploit natural resources in the occupied territories.

October 1991

The Madrid (Spain) Peace Conference includes delegations from Israel, Syria, Jordan, Lebanon, Egypt, and the Palestinians. It marks the first time most of the Arab parties (except for Egypt) and Israel sat down at a table together. The conference is organized along bi-lateral [involving or participated in by two nations] lines as well as multilateral [participated in by more than two nations] lines.

January–September 1993

Secret talks between Israeli Prime Minister Yitzhak Rabin and PLO leader Yasser Arafat begin in Oslo, Norway. September: they sign a Declaration of Principles in Washington on the basis of the negotiations made in Oslo.

Israel recognized the PLO and gave them limited autonomy (in the occupied territories of the West Bank and Gaza) in return for peace.	*The PLO in turn gave up its claims to Israel's territory as defined by its borders before the 1967 war. The Palestinians also agreed to end the Intifada and establish security in the West Bank and Gaza.*

- The trade-offs made became known as "land for peace." Because they could not resolve all the issues right away, the two sides agreed to make gradual steps towards a final settlement of the conflict. The process by which the two sides would gradually exchange land for peace and work out the more difficult issues standing in the way of a final agreement became known as the "Oslo peace process."
- The two sides were no longer claiming that the other did not have the right to exist as a state or peoples on that land and both pledged to work towards a final agreement that would settle all outstanding issues between them.

103

Authority sign a revised deal based on the stalled Wye River accord, aimed at reviving the Middle East peace process.

November: final status talks resume between Israel and the Palestinians.

2000

February: a summit between Barak and Palestinian leader Yasser Arafat breaks up over a disagreement on a promised Israeli withdrawal from the West Bank under the revised Wye accord. Final status negotiations between Israel and the Palestinians are deadlocked as the deadline for a framework agreement [basic guidelines for an eventual final agreement for peace between Palestinians and Israelis] is missed. In March, Israel hands over part of the West Bank to Palestinians as part of a land transfer agreed to at the Wye River conferences of 1998. The land amounted to 6.1% of the total of the West Bank.

May: unilaterally withdraws from the area of Lebanon it was occupying since 1982.

July: a peace summit between Palestinian and Israeli leaders and negotiators at Camp David ends deadlocked over competing claims to Jerusalem and the issue of Palestinians refugees. Palestinians and Israelis accused each other of not being willing to make the compromises necessary for an agreement.

Israel believes its offer of handing over 95% of the West Bank and Gaza to Palestinians for the formation of a Palestinian state to be generous. Israel views its condition of maintaining control over settlements and security zones in the West Bank to be not only reasonable but also necessary for its national security.	*Palestinians believe they should not have to accept less than 100% of the West Bank and Gaza because the total of both territories only comprises 22% of what was originally Palestine. Palestinians also view the Israeli proposal as unacceptable because it would divide the Palestinian state into disconnected regions; a situation that would not free them from Israeli occupation and would not make for a truly independent state.*

September: Ariel Sharon, the leader of Likud [Israel's right-wing political party], visits the Temple Mount, known to Muslims as the Haram al-Sharif ("Noble Sanctuary") with 1,000 Israeli soldiers. A Palestinian protest of Sharon's visit turns violent and sparks demonstrations and violence that have continued until today.

Sharon and his supporters state that the Palestinian violence was planned before his visit to the Temple Mount and that the Palestinians are only using his visit to the Mount as an excuse for their attacks. The Israeli Ministry of Foreign Affairs has used the term "Terror Intifada" to describe the violence committed by Palestinians since September 2001. Israelis point to Palestinian attacks on Joseph's tomb (in West Bank town of Nablus) on October 8th, 2000 and Rachel's tomb (in West Bank town of Bethlehem) as proof that Palestinians do not respect Jewish holy sites and therefore should not be granted sovereignty over the Temple Mount.	*Because Jews do not normally visit the Temple Mount except as tourists and because Sharon made his visit accompanied by 1,000 soldiers during a delicate part of the peace process, Sharon has been criticized for trying to provoke a Palestinian reaction that would undermine the peace process. Palestinians term their demonstrations and attacks the "al-Aqsa Intifada," in the name of the mosque on the Haram al-Sharif and state that the Intifada is fueled by frustration over continued Israeli occupation of the majority of the West Bank and parts of the Gaza Strip.*

Al Aqsa Intifada marks the first time Palestinian citizens of Israel have participated in protests and demonstrations against Israel in solidarity with Palestinians in the West Bank and Gaza.

Israelis cite the participation of Arab Israelis in the recent Intifada as a reason not to allow Palestinian refugees to return to live in Israel.	*Arab Israelis have stated that they are protesting the continued occupation of the West Bank and the Gaza Strip as well as the treatment of Arab Israelis within Israel. According to the Nazareth-based Arab Association for Human Rights, there are huge gaps in local government budgets for Jewish and Arab towns and municipalities.*

October: Clinton presides over a summit between Palestinians and Israelis at the Egyptian resort of Sharm el-Sheikh. The summit attendees announce a cease-fire and plans to bring an end to the Palestinian-Israeli violence but the cease-fire comes undone soon after it is formed. With his governing coalition teetering on the edge of collapse, Israeli Prime Minister Ehud Barak gives his resignation to the country's president in December, stating that he wants to seek a new mandate from the Israeli people. In other words, he hoped to get re-elected on the platform of continuing to work towards a final peace agreement with the Palestinians, and thereby regain the authority to take the steps necessary to achieve such an agreement. Barak ran as the Labor Party's candidate against Likud Party candidate Ariel Sharon.

February: Likud Party (Israel's right wing) candidate Ariel Sharon is elected as Prime Minister of Israel beating Ehud Barak by more than 20 percentage points. Sharon campaigned on the platform of "Peace with Security," and promised that he would take a different approach to the Palestinian conflict than the Oslo Peace Process approach. Palestinians are long-time critics of Ariel Sharon because of his role in Israel's 1982 invasion of Lebanon, and his support of Israel's settlement activity.

February 2001

Following the deaths of eight soldiers and civilians killed when a Palestinian bus driver ploughed his vehicle into a waiting line of passengers, Israel reimposes a total blockade on the occupied territories.	Palestinians claim that the blockades prevent medical and humanitarian supplies from reaching Palestinians and prevent Palestinians from attending their jobs in Israel and traveling between towns in the occupied territories.

March: Ariel Sharon formally takes office as Israeli prime minister, heading a fragile seven party coalition and a government team comprising a third of the 120-member Knesset. Veteran Labor leader Shimon Peres serves as Foreign Minister, after talking his party into joining Ariel Sharon's rightwing government of national unity. In April, Israeli troops seize territory controlled by the Palestinians for the first time since the start of the Oslo process. Israeli troops seize the Gaza Strip and divide the territory into three parts.

May: the Mitchell Commission calls for an immediate ceasefire, to be followed by confidence building measures and ultimately by renewed peace negotiations. Mitchell also calls for a freeze on expansion of Jewish settlements in the occupied territories. Additionally, the European Union accuses Israel of using "disproportionate" force in the occupied territories and calls on it to dismantle Jewish settlements in the West Bank and Gaza Strip.

June: a suicide bomber kills 19 young Israelis at a nightclub in Tel Aviv. Yasser Arafat orders his forces in the occupied territories to enforce a ceasefire.

July: the Israeli security cabinet votes to give the Israeli Defense Forces (IDF) a broader license to target Palestinian terrorists. Formerly, the IDF was only permitted to assassinate terrorists actually on their way to committing an attack. The new guidelines allow the IDF to act against known terrorists even if they are not on the verge of committing an attack.

Israel has stated that it must undertake preventive action against imminent terrorist threats and that in the small minority of cases where arrests are impossible (mostly due to the lack of Israeli jurisdiction in PA areas), it is forced to carry out other types of preventative operations it terms "active self-defense." Israel states that international law in general, and the law of armed conflict in particular, recognize that individuals who directly take part in hostilities cannot claim immunity from attack or protection as innocent	Palestinians have taken issue with Israel's policy of "targeted assassinations," stating that these killings constitute extra-judicial executions, where the victims have been killed without trial and without the chance of a fair legal process designed to examine the allegations brought forward against them. Palestinians state that under the Fourth Geneva Convention, Israel as the Occupying Power has the right to arrest and bring to trial those suspected of violent hostile activities. However, under the same Convention, extra-

civilians. Israel states that it only acts in a manner that is in compliance with the principles and practice of armed conflict, and makes every effort to avoid involvement of innocent civilians.	*judicial executions are willful killings, which constitute war crimes and are subject to universal jurisdiction.*

August: in retaliation for a Jerusalem suicide bombing on the previous day, Israeli warplanes fire missiles at and level the headquarters of the Palestinian police in the West Bank city of Ramallah. The militant Islamist group Hamas claimed responsibility for the bombing. Israeli Special Forces also seize the offices of the Palestine Liberation Organization at Orient House in East Jerusalem. Several days later, Israeli tanks move into the West Bank city of Jenin and open fire on the Palestinian police station, destroying it. This is the biggest incursion into Palestinian controlled territory since 1994. The move is strongly criticized by Washington, which is coming under increasing international pressure to step up its intermediary role in the region. Nevertheless, on Israeli troops move into the West Bank town of Beit Jala, near the southern outskirts of Jerusalem. The U.S. and Britain strongly condemn the Israeli action.

Late Summer and Fall: Israel occupies major Palestinian cities for various lengths of time, including Jerico, Ramallah and Tulkarm.

Though the Israeli-Palestinian conflict has escalated since the October 17th, 2001 assassination of the Israeli hard-line Tourism Minister Rehavam Zeevi by Palestinian militants, there are positive signs of a renewed interest in peace talks. In a speech to the United Nations on November 15th, Israeli Foreign Minister Shimon Peres spoke of Israeli support for Palestinian independence and a Palestinian state.

Since the terrorist attacks on New York and Washington, D.C. of September 11th, the Bush administration has shown more of an interest in bringing Israel and the Palestinians to negotiations, greatly in response to requests from Arab and Muslim governments that are supporting the U.S. war against terrorism. On October 2, Bush announced a dramatic break with his administration's previous Middle East policy by stating that he is prepared to back the creation of a Palestinian state and U.S. Secretary of State Colin Powell is expected to outline a new American initiative for restoring negotiations between Israel and Palestine.

Assignment Part Two:
- Read the 14 italicized segments that contrast the Israeli and Palestinian perspectives on the same issues.
- Find 5 segments that show the greatest contrast in perspective and complete the following chart.

Example:

Name of the event	Israeli Perspective	Palestinian Perspective
Balfour Declaration: Creation of a homeland for Jews in British occupied Palestine.	Zionists are happy to have a homeland. They feel great allegiance to the British who helped them secure this location.	Concerned that they are losing their territory. Do not want to be under the rule of the British or the Jews. Want to pursue a unified Arab state that encompasses the Middle East. Willing to compromise with the British to secure their independence.

Attachment 14: Resolution 242

Decisions

At its 1373rd meeting, on 9 November 1967, the Council decided to invite the representatives of the United Arab Republic, Israel and Jordan to participate, without vote, in the discussion of the item entitled "The situation in the Middle East: Letter dated 7 November 1967 from the Permanent Representative of the United Arab Republic addressed to the President of the Security Council (S/8226)".[11]

At its 1375th meeting, on 13 November 1967, the Council decided to invite the representative of Syria to participate, without vote, in the discussion of the question.

Resolution 242 (1967)

of 22 November 1967

The Security Council,

Expressing its continuing concern with the grave situation in the Middle East,

Emphasizing the inadmissibility of the acquisition of territory by war and the need to work for a just and lasting peace in which every State in the area can live in security,

Emphasizing further that all Member States in their acceptance of the Charter of the United Nations have undertaken a commitment to act in accordance with Article 2 of the Charter,

1. *Affirms* that the fulfilment of Charter principles requires the establishment of a just and lasting peace in the Middle East which should include the application of both the following principles:

   (i) Withdrawal of Israel armed forces from territories occupied in the recent conflict;

   (ii) Termination of all claims or states of belligerency and respect for and acknowledgement of the sovereignty, territorial integrity and political independence of every State in the area and their right to live in peace within secure and recognized boundaries free from threats or acts of force;

2. *Affirms further* the necessity

   (a) For guaranteeing freedom of navigation through international waterways in the area;

   (b) For achieving a just settlement of the refugee problem;

   (c) For guaranteeing the territorial inviolability and political independence of every State in the area,

through measures including the establishment of demilitarized zones;

3. *Requests* the Secretary-General to designate a Special Representative to proceed to the Middle East to establish and maintain contacts with the States concerned in order to promote agreement and assist efforts to achieve a peaceful and accepted settlement in accordance with the provisions and principles in this resolution;

4. *Requests* the Secretary-General to report to the Security Council on the progress of the efforts of the Special Representative as soon as possible.

Adopted unanimously at the 1382nd meeting.

Decision

On 8 December 1967, the following statement which reflected the view of the members of the Council was circulated by the President as a Security Council document (S/8289):[12]

"As regards document S/8053/Add.3,[12] brought to the attention of the Security Council, the members, recalling the consensus reached at its 1366th meeting on 9 July 1967, recognize the necessity of the enlargement by the Secretary-General of the number of observers in the Suez Canal zone and the provision of additional technical material and means of transportation."

THE CYPRUS QUESTION[13]

Decision

At its 1362nd meeting, on 19 June 1967, the Council decided to invite the representatives of Cyprus, Turkey and Greece to participate, without vote, in the discussion of the item entitled "Letter dated 26 December 1963 from the Permanent Representative of Cyprus addressed to the President of the Security Council (S/5488):[14] report of the Secretary-General on the United Nations Operation in Cyprus (S/7969)".[15]

[11] *Ibid.*

[12] *Ibid.*

[13] Resolutions or decisions on this question were also adopted in 1963, 1964, 1965 and 1966.

[14] See *Official Records of the Security Council, Eighteenth Year, Supplement for October, November and December 1963.*

[15] *Ibid., Twenty-second Year, Supplement for April, May and June 1967.*

Unit Six: Towards a Peaceful Solution: The Arab/Israeli Conflict (1948-2013)

<u>Essential Questions</u>
• Historically, what factors have aggravated the relationship between Israelis and Arabs? What factors have allowed for negotiation, peace, and co-existence?
• In regards to the Israeli/Palestinian conflict today, what are the most viable prospects for peace and the most serious concerns for conflict?

<u>Due Friday, April 5th : Introduction to the Arab/Israeli Conflict</u>
Read: *Arab-Israeli Timeline* from *PBS.org*, "Origins of the Dispute" by James Gelvin
Consider: Comprehensively outline the relationship between Israel and its *neighboring countries* between 1948 and the present. What conditions fueled conflict and what conditions allowed for peace to be made?
Consider: Comprehensively outline the relationship between the Israelis and the *Palestinians* between 1948 and the present. What conditions fueled conflict and what conditions allowed for peace to be made?

<u>Due Monday, April 8th : Understanding the History of Political Diversity in Israel and the Palestinian Territories</u>
Note: Despite the order of the documents in the PDF file, read the documents in chronological order.
Read: Israeli Declaration of Independence (1947), Palestinian National Charter (1968), "We Recognize Israel " by Yasir Arafat (1988), "Charter of the Islamic Resistance Movement" by Hamas (1988), "The Price of Occupation" by Yitzak Rabin (1994), "Program for Dealing with the Palestinians" by Ariel Sharon (2000)
Consider: Identify the similarities and differences between the Israeli Declaration of Independence and the Palestinian National Charter. Are the goals defined in these charters negotiable or irreconcilable?
Consider: After reading the last four documents, identify the similarities and differences between each point of view and consider whether or not the differences can be reconciled?

<u>Due Tuesday, April 9th: Understanding the Current Israeli and Palestinian Political Establishment</u>
Read: "Israel Country Profile" from *BBC*, "Palestinian Territories Profile" from *BBC*, 'Hawks' Wings are Clipped" from *The Economist*, "Q&A: Israel's New Government" from the *BBC*, "Fatah Profile" from *BBC*, "Hamas Profile" from *BBC*
Consider: What are some of the political challenges facing both political establishments today, internally or otherwise?
Consider: How might the current political landscape affect the chances for a one or two-state solution?

<u>Due Thursday, April 11th: Understanding Political Diversity in the Arab/Israeli Conflict</u>
Complete: Israeli / Palestinian Conflict Simulation Materials distributed in class

<u>Due Friday, April 12th : Peace-Making and the Two State Solution</u>
In-Class: Prominent Voices on the One vs. Two State Solution

Enjoy your April Vacation!